Special Praise for
The Road to Shine

"With honesty, clarity, and compassion, Laurie teaches us how to trust our inner wisdom to reach new levels of happiness and peace."

—**Katherine K. Merseth**
Coauthor of *Inside Urban Charter Schools*
Director, Teacher Education Program
Harvard Graduate School of Education

"*The Road to Shine* exemplifies awareness in action. Laurie Gardner's collection of personal experiences can inspire you to claim your passion and live in harmony with your authentic self."

—**Bob Olson**
Coauthor of *Understanding Spirit, Understanding Yourself*
Founder, BestPsychicDirectory.com
OfSpirit.com Magazine
AfterLifeTV.com

"Laurie Gardner is a delightful storyteller. She shares her journey through self-doubt and self-judgment toward a true shining of spirit—with vulnerability, humanity, and hard-earned insight. For those seeking to shine, this book can be a great friend."

—**Donald Rothberg**
Author of *The Engaged Spiritual Life*
Teacher, Spirit Rock Meditation Center

The
Road
to Shine

The
Road
to Shine

A Story of Adventure, Life Lessons,
and My Quest for More

Laurie Gardner

CENTRAL RECOVERY PRESS

Las Vegas

Central Recovery Press (CRP) is committed to publishing exceptional materials addressing addiction treatment, recovery, and behavioral healthcare topics, including original and quality books, audio/visual communications, and web-based new media. Through a diverse selection of titles, we seek to contribute a broad range of unique resources for professionals, recovering individuals and their families, and the general public.

For more information, visit www.centralrecoverypress.com.

Publisher: Central Recovery Press
3321 N. Buffalo Drive
Las Vegas, NV 89129

19 18 17 16 15 14   1 2 3 4 5

ISBN: 978-1-937612-59-7 (paper)
978-1-937612-60-3 (e-book)

Publisher's Note: This is a memoir, a work based on fact recorded to the best of the author's memory. To protect their privacy, the names of some of the people, places, and institutions in this book have been changed.

Central Recovery Press books represent the experiences and opinions of their authors only. Every effort has been made to ensure that events, institutions, and statistics presented in our books as facts are accurate and up-to-date.

Cover design and interior by Deb Tremper, Six Penny Graphics.
Frontispiece Map by Jack Laws, Jamie Does, James Harwell, and Laurie Gardner.
Author photo by Bob Lasky. Used with permission.

This book is for all who sense there's something more.
May you discover just how brightly you can shine.

And for Jack.
I couldn't have done this without you.

Table of Contents

ACKNOWLEDGMENTS

It would be impossible to thank in just a few words all of the amazing people who were an integral part of this project and who've helped to shape who I am and where I am today. While I don't have room to list everyone by name, know that I deeply love and appreciate you all.

To my close friends and extended family, for being my support and sounding board through all of my transformations. To my wise teachers and mentors, your sage advice has guided me well. To those who believed in me and cheered me on, even when I doubted myself. To my gifted team of experts: my fabulous editors, Leigh Haber, Christina Williamson, and Eliza Tutellier; my stellar agent, Bill Gladstone; my fairy godfathers, Rick and Scott Frishman; the talented crew at CRP; my sharp cookie legal counselors, Jonathan Horn, Marc Paisin, and Steve Hirschfeld; and my wonderful website wizards, Isai Torres Garcia and Michael Montgomery. Last, but definitely not least, to my family, Barbara, Allan, Alisa, and Adam. Though I've often caused you worry with my crazy adventures, you've always been there for me, loving me enough to let me be me.

INTRODUCTION

Virtually every country has an expression that means, "Life is short; don't waste it."

"Wasted time makes the saints cry." (Guatemala)

"Eat and drink for tomorrow we die." (Israel)

"Life is found in taking the opportunity." (China)

And, popular among the US social media crowd:

"YOLO" ("You Only Live Once").

Since we all seem to agree that life is a precious gift, why do so many people settle for less? Too many work in jobs they don't like, stay in unfulfilling relationships, live where they don't feel at home, and maintain less-than-ideal health. Others feel content in many ways, but still sense that something's missing.

Many of us know the expression "hiding your light under a bushel," yet we're often unaware when we're doing it ourselves. Even if you don't realize you're keeping yourself small, deep down you know when you're not really happy. Maybe you're feeling depleted or detached around your loved ones. Perhaps you're bored or overextended at work. Maybe you've never felt settled where you live, or you generally feel that something's not quite right. Chances are, if you're picking up a book called *The Road to Shine*, some part of you knows there's more to life than what you've been living.

How do we define happiness anyway? For me, it's not a temporary state, like when we drink a glass of wine or win a prize and feel good in the moment but then go back to a crappy life. True happiness is the deep, existential contentment that arises when our outer world matches who we are internally; in other words, when what we're doing, who we're with, and how we're being in the world reflects who we really are. When the two worlds match, happiness can sometimes be experienced as elation and euphoria, at other times as a grounded sense of peace. The key is that it lasts; it's on our soul level, not just a passing mood or feeling.

When our inner and outer worlds match, we're maximizing our authentic selves, "being all we can be." In the words of humanist psychologist Abraham Maslow, we're fully "self-actualizing."

But *how* can we stop settling for less and start making the most of our lives?

This was my burning question as I sat high on a desert cliff one blistering summer seven years ago. While fasting alone on a vision quest for four days, a book came pouring out into my leather journal, outlining three steps to living more fully:

1. Uncover and heal your lack of self-love.
2. Discover or remember your passion and purpose.
3. Find the courage to shine.

As I looked back at my own life, I realized that these steps must be gone through in order. You can't jump right to living your passion if you haven't first cleaned up the deeper stuff that's holding you back.

I understood that these words not only represented the stages of my own path, but that they could also guide others. As my desert download continued, I expanded the steps into a three-part road map, adding landmarks and practical tips to move through each stage. The message was straightforward: If you follow this, you'll be much happier. If you don't, your life will continue to feel flat.

Shortly after returning from my vision quest, a major New York publisher expressed interest in what I'd written and urged me to share my personal journey through the three steps. Part of me wanted to respond (in my best Monty Python accent), "I'm not dead yet!" Weren't memoirs written by people who had lived long lives and were practically dead? Either that, or by people who had done something pretty amazing to write about themselves at such a young age. But after my editor's suggestion sunk in a little deeper, I decided that if writing a memoir could potentially help others, it was certainly worth a try.

So it is with great humility and tremendous gratitude that I offer this story of my own road to shine. I picked lessons and experiences that almost all of us go through in one form or another, sharing them with the hope that some pieces will resonate in just the right way to inspire others to find more fulfillment in their own lives. If, after reading this book, even one person concludes, "Well, if she could do it, so can I," I will have accomplished my goal.

A word of caution: The road to shine is not for the faint of heart. The journey is fraught with brutal self-honesty leading to exhilarating transformation. It's important to be patient with yourself; you'll progress at whatever pace your unique expedition is meant to unfold. In the end, I don't know of a single person who has regretted the trip.

Journey well, bright lights.

I

WHY AM I HERE?

Burning sage smells like marijuana.

That's not a very reverent thought to have during a sacred ceremony as you're being purified with a plant that's holy to Native Americans. I can't help it, though; the scent is exactly the same as the back of my old school bus.

"I'd like each of you to share why you've decided to go on a vision quest," says Sparrow, our group leader. Two people in the circle cross and uncross their legs nervously. Others stare thoughtfully up at the sky.

Why *did* I want to go on a vision quest? What in God's name possessed me to sign up for two weeks in the desert in the heat of summer, including fasting alone in the wilderness for four days and four nights? I can barely make it to dinner when I skip lunch; how am I going to stop eating for almost a week?

I don't even really know what a vision quest is. Neither does anyone else in my immediate circle of friends and family, though they have some interesting ideas.

"Don't hurt yourself while doing those psychedelic drugs."

"Careful about sunburn while you wander around naked."

"Aren't you nervous about being isolated in the wilderness with criminal kids?"

My mom mailed me a newspaper clipping of a corporate group visioning out its goals in an executive boardroom, with a sticky note saying, "Have fun!"

So far, my vision quest is nothing like anyone's expectations. Ben, a jovial man with an easy grin and warm handshake, introduces himself first. "I'm here as part of my twelve-step program, to overcome my addiction to overeating."

Susan has a dimpled smile but sad eyes. Wiping away tears, she recounts the recent death of her partner and says, "I'm hoping to find a way to move on."

Ted is an eager, new college graduate who looks about sixteen years old. He tells us, "There are so many different choices in the world! I want to figure out what to do with my life."

Bill, a successful but life-weary artist, exhales heavily and says, "I hope this vision quest helps me find a renewed sense of purpose."

When it's Faith's turn, she begins passionately, "I just adore my beautiful children and love raising them!" Then her voice becomes soft. "But I've lost my identity outside of being a mother. I came here to remember who I am."

The woman next to her looks like she's on the verge of sprinting out of the circle and as far away from the group as possible. "My name is Julie. I've recently stopped doing drugs, but I still hate myself." She shifts uncomfortably in her seat, grateful when the next person chimes in.

Karen is a young doctoral student in her twenties. "I'm way too much in my head," she tells us. "I want to get back in touch with my emotions."

Across the circle, Annie is making little piles of dirt all around her like miniature sand castles, quietly delighting in her own creations.

When it's her turn, she says, "I think I've been in my computer programming job for too long; I've forgotten how to play."

"And you, Laurie?" Sparrow prompts me.

Wow, what can I say? The thing is, I don't have one big issue I want to overcome, like a death or addiction, or just one uplifting goal, like learning to play. My reason for being here is messier than that. My life has been a cycle of ups and downs, of outward success and inward pain, a complex brew of near unbearable sadness and ecstatic joy, sometimes in succession and sometimes all at the same time.

Growing up wasn't easy for me. My best years were my college days and my twenties. I felt so alive then—adventurous, open, and free. In my thirties, I somehow lost all that, diving into a deeper darkness than any I'd experienced before.

Back in the circle, all eyes are on me, waiting for me to speak.

How can I sum up in one brief statement how numb and frozen I've been over the last ten years, my recent "thawing" process, and my intense desire to return to who I really am, to that person who's so passionate and happy?

Maybe I should just blurt out everything I'm going through: I'm sick and tired of wearing a "happy mask" when I'm actually sad inside. I hate feeling hurt and wounded all the time; my anger and pain are exhausting. I'm tired of being a workaholic, distracting myself from my pain. I take everything too personally and constantly beat myself up or get defensive. I'm tired of opening up to people, then being betrayed by them. I don't trust anyone anymore. I feel disconnected from everyone and everything. I'm tired of people criticizing and judging me, and me judging and criticizing them and myself. I want to meet my soul mate, but I'm afraid I'm so guarded from all the times I've been hurt that I won't be able to let him in. I want to know where I'm going in life, and I'm fed up with fear holding me back from being all I can be. Basically, I don't feel lovable or worthy a lot of the time, and I'm freakin' sick of it!

How did I get to this point?

2

⁘

THE HARVARD HOBO

Whose Kid Is This?
Follow Your Bliss, Even If Other People Don't Approve

A week after I graduated from college, my parents sat me down in the family living room, looking anxious and perplexed. I had just announced that I was leaving to backpack around the world by myself. I had no set itinerary or pre-arranged destinations; my only plan was that I would explore for at least a year.

"Just tell us why!" My mother buried her head in her hands, as if I had just killed someone.

Looking at me earnestly, my father said, "You graduated with high honors. You won a fellowship to the American University in Cairo, and you have a job offer from your German professor. Is this really what you want to do?"

Clearly, my parents weren't as excited about the idea as I was.

"How are you going to pay for this?" my mom asked.

"I've got a summer job leading a group of high school students on an exchange trip through New Zealand and Australia. My flights and expenses are all paid, and I can extend my return ticket for up to a year. After the kids leave, I'll stay and see where the winds blow me."

"But how will we get in touch with you?" She shot a worried look at my dad.

There were no cell phones yet and no Internet cafes for the wayward traveler.

"I could fax you once a month to let you know where I am and that I'm okay."

"Once a week."

"Once every two weeks."

"Deal," my dad said, patting my mom on the shoulder.

⌒

Two months later, I was sitting on a bunk bed in a youth hostel in Christchurch, the largest city on the South Island of New Zealand. As I kicked off my shoes, the magnitude of my decision hit me: I was out in the world alone, indefinitely.

When I was ten, I went to a sleep-away camp in Vermont for two months, my first time being away from home for more than a night. I missed my house and parents so much that, one day, I just walked out of the arts and crafts shed and through the camp's main gate. "I can make it home to New Jersey from here," my little ten-year-old self decided determinedly. I was a mile down the road before they found me.

My stomach cramped with nausea as a wave of intense loneliness and fear passed through me. *Maybe I should just go home and look for a job. What am I going to do out here? Where will I go? What the hell was I thinking?*

My bunkmate had a wine bottle with a thick, woolen sock over it strapped to her backpack.

"What's with the wooly wine?" I asked.

"I just came back from working on a sheep farm that's also a vineyard. Want the number?"

~

"So, can you cook?" asked the voice on the phone in a thick New Zealand accent.

"Yes sir."

"Do you ride horses?"

"Not in years, but I used to ride quite a bit as a kid. Did show jumping and everything."

"How soon can you start?"

"As soon as you like, sir."

"Call me John. I'll pick you up in an hour."

A lean, swaggering man in his fifties wearing oily work coveralls and gumboots pulled up in front of the youth hostel in a white Ford pick-up truck.

He rolled down his window and asked, "Can you stay for at least a month? I need a head farmhand."

"I don't see why not," I said.

We drove due north into the countryside, a seemingly endless landscape of rolling, green hills dotted with white fluffy sheep, mirror images of the clouds overhead. As we chatted, I wasn't sure what to make of John. With social conversation, he was very curt, cutting right to the point of what he needed to know without any of the usual niceties. But just when I'd decided he was a man of few words, I asked him about New Zealand's politics, and he went off on a lengthy, fervent rant that lasted the rest of the forty-five minutes until we arrived at his farm.

"Come on," he said, jumping out of the truck and onto a dubious looking motorbike with the muffler tied on with a piece of white rope. "Hop on!"

I held on for dear life as we raced through a lumpy paddock full of dozens of sheep.

"You see that one over there?"

"Yeah."

"Get off and throw it over the fence; it's not mine."

"Uhhhh . . ."

He drove off, leaving me in the middle of the field.

I chased that stupid sheep around for a good fifteen minutes before John returned, laughing and shaking his head. "Aw look, you've got to grab it around the neck to put it into submission."

Sure enough, as soon as I managed to get put my hands around its throat in a stranglehold, it dropped to the ground, looking up at me for mercy.

"Good on ya'! Now throw it over."

I don't know how much the average sheep weighs, but I couldn't even lift this one off the ground, never mind toss it over a five-foot fence. Laughing again, John grabbed it with one arm and threw it over the fence. It landed with a thud on its side, then scrambled to its feet.

"Let's go," John said, "I want you to meet Marg."

We drove past several more sheep paddocks, various feed crops, and a few pens of cattle before arriving at the vineyard. Rows of grapevines stretched for acres toward the horizon, looking like leafy lane lines in a giant green swimming pool. A stout woman emerged from the middle of the third row of vines. She was about John's age with short hair tucked into a bright pink knit cap.

"I'm Marg; g'day mate," she said with a grunt, extending a dirt-stained hand.

"Well, I'll leave you to it," John said, and left.

He sure wasn't spending much time showing me the ropes. I didn't mind. I'd just eaten a big meal a couple of hours ago; it was warm and sunny, and Marg seemed nice enough.

"So what is it we're doing out here, Marg?"

"Tending the vines," she said, pointing to the new, wayward shoots not yet attached to the wire. "The trick is, you've got to get the twist tie on there just right. Then you've got to crouch real low and check each of these irrigation drips at the bottom of the base to make sure a rabbit didn't chew it off."

After about twenty minutes, Marg announced, "Time for a cuppa!" She pulled out a thermos and offered me a sip of tea. Then she pulled out a raw onion sandwich from her shirt pocket, took a couple of bites, and let out a tremendous belch.

"More tea?" She extended the thermos toward me, with a piece of onion hanging out of her mouth.

"Uh, no thanks."

"Well, that's enough work for today," she said, taking off her gloves. We couldn't have been there for more than an hour. On the drive there, John had told me he preferred hiring foreigners because "they work damn harder than the Kiwis." He seemed to have a point.

The sun was getting lower in the sky, and I was in charge of making dinner. "I'd best be getting to the house, Marg," I said. "See you tomorrow?"

"You bet, see you bright and early—well, not too early."

BANG! A shot rang out on the front porch. I was so startled I dropped the cookbook I had been browsing. A moment later, John came into the kitchen, carrying a rabbit by the ears that was dripping with blood.

"Cook 'er up into a stew," he said, pushing it toward me.

"Not on your life!" I squealed.

At first he looked angry, then he grinned. "All right, I'll give it to the dogs. Do you know how to make shortbread?"

"Desserts are my specialty," I smiled.

When I was a kid, nothing made me happier than whipping up a fresh batch of brownies while belting out show tunes. Although I no longer had aspirations of becoming a singing pastry chef, cooking for John was the next best thing. He went through plates of my shortbread like they were handfuls of peanuts. Each day, I'd come in from the fields or vines an hour early, crank the radio, and sing at the top of my lungs as I prepared dinner and another round of cookies.

John McCaskey was quite a character: A short-tempered yet good-natured fellow who muttered curses under his breath on the tractor and laughed at his own dirty jokes. A lanky, Scottish immigrant, he loved playing the saxophone as much as he loved working the land.

One day, John called me down to the sheep barn. "Can you hold steady under pressure?" he asked.

I must've looked worried, because he added, "Don't worry, you don't have to castrate any more lambs."

He escorted me into the main barn, where the temperature was at least 100 degrees. There was a team of husky, sweating men with clippers, shearing the wool off the sheep in record time.

"We got a lot of sheep to get through today, and your job is to keep 'em moving. Get under the barn and push the sheep up the chute. When you're done with a round of sheep, run back up here, get the wool from the shearers' feet, and throw it in that tall burlap bin over there. When the sack is full, stomp it all down and sew it up with that twine. Got all that?"

I must have lost ten pounds that day, slapping sheep on the butt from under the barn, running up to the shearing stage to clear the wool, jumping into the burlap sacks up to my knees, and then hustling back under the barn. The men let me try my hand at shearing during the lunch break, and it was much harder than it looked. By the time we stopped at ten o'clock that night, we were all sweaty and exhausted, but also elated.

"Good work, mates!" John said, clapping the shearers on the back. "Pub time!"

Marge Piercy wrote a powerful poem called, "To Be of Use" about jumping in the trenches and getting done what needs to be done. That's exactly what I loved about being on John's farm. "Fence post needs fixing? No problem!" "Irrigation system not working? I'll figure it out." "Snip the dirty wool off the legs of 900 sheep? I'm on it!"

I didn't want to just skim along or hang out in life; I wanted to *contribute*. I needed to feel like my life had a purpose. This drive for meaning and purpose started when I was sixteen years old.

The summer before my high school senior year, I was an exchange student on a Swiss farm. While most kids back home were filling out college applications and stressing about the SATs, I was happily milking cows and hoping that my cute blond host brother would notice me.

For the first time in my life, I felt completely at ease, living in a peaceful, beautiful countryside surrounded by kind, authentic people. Living directly off the land felt so natural and "right." Every morning, I awoke at dawn for the 5:00 a.m. milking. Walking barefoot down the cobblestone street of our village to the local dairy, I would exchange my buckets of fresh milk for a large wheel of cheese and some newly pressed butter. Stopping at the bakery on the way home, I'd pick out a loaf of country bread that was still warm. Before walking inside the farmhouse, I'd graze my way through the patch of overgrown fruits and vegetables next to the shed, hoping not to get busted by my host mother. Dori was a powerful, imposing woman whose generous, but no-nonsense attitude had earned her widespread respect as the matriarch of the village.

"Laurie, as-tu mangé dans le jardin encore?" ("Laurie, did you eat in the garden again?")

"Moi? Mais non!" ("Me? Of course not!") I protested, with blackberry stains around my mouth.

"Qu'est-ce qu'on va faire avec toi?" ("What are we going to do with you?") Laughing, she wiped her hands on her apron.

⌒

One evening, sitting high on my favorite hillside, listening to the tinkling of cowbells on the patchwork of fields below, I wrote my first song, called, "Who am I?" Strumming along with my host brother's guitar, I crooned out soul-searching questions about life and my place in it, as only a teenager can. Soon, I'd be finishing high school and have to decide what to do with my life.

In Switzerland, people choose at age twelve or thirteen what they want to be when they grow up. Based on that decision, they're either officially finished with school a few years later, or they begin an academic track toward their chosen career. My nine-year-old host cousin already knew that he wanted to be a farmer like his dad. His eleven-year-old brother wanted to be an aeronautic engineer.

Both boys' decisions were received with open praise and enthusiasm. No one looked down on the younger son for wanting to work a blue collar job, and no one scorned the oldest son for not carrying on the family tradition. In their culture, children were encouraged to follow their dreams, whatever they might be. These values made complete sense to me. I saw no point in going back to the American rat race.

"I'm going to live here for the rest of my life!" I informed my parents the day before I was scheduled to fly back home to New Jersey.

My parents balked, then made me an offer I couldn't refuse. "If you go to college now, you can travel every summer."

Surprise! It's Me!
Welcome Your Passion When It
Shows Up Out of Nowhere

The Harvard undergraduate course catalog was the size of a phone book. I'd gone from having very limited choices while growing up to so many options, it was overwhelming. Two weeks before classes began, I was hiking up Mount Monadnock in New Hampshire on a freshmen orientation camping trip. Our hiking leader was a senior, so I thought I'd pick her brain.

"You should check out Diana Eck's comparative world religions class," she said.

"Um, okay . . . thanks."

What I was thinking is, *Uh, no thanks.* I had little interest in religion. I was raised in a liberal, reform Jewish family that celebrated the High Holidays and Passover—sort of like Christian families who go to church only on Christmas and Easter. Mostly, my family enjoyed the cultural aspects of Judaism, especially eating large quantities of home-cooked food with loved ones. Outside of reading prayers during holiday services, there was no mention of any sort of "God." I had no idea if anyone in my family even believed in one.

Culturally, I was raised a WASP (White Anglo-Saxon Protestant). My family was one of only a few Jewish families in our tiny rural town where the deer outnumbered the people three to one. For those who remember the popular *Preppy Handbook* of the 1980s, those Muffys and Biffs in the bright pink Izods were my peers. I was the preppy who carried the lime green Bermuda bag but who occasionally ate latkes.

It wasn't easy being one of the few Jewish kids in school.

"Where are your horns?" asked Evan, the boy who sat behind me in fourth grade.

"My mom says that Jews have horns because they killed Jesus."

"I don't have any horns!" I said, blushing.

When the head of the junior high cheerleaders found out I was Jewish, she nicknamed me "Hanny" for Hanukkah. For years, kids refused to call me by my real name.

One morning, I came running into class one minute before the bell rang and slid into my seat. As I put down my notebook, I noticed that someone had carved a swastika on my desk.

⌢

When it was time to enroll, my trip leader's suggestion kept niggling at my brain. Finally, I decided to give the religion class a go.

When I walked in on the first day, I half expected to be welcomed by burning incense and meditation cushions in place of desks. Instead, I found a diverse, but fairly normal looking group. There were a few stand-outs: a bald, Burmese monk in a saffron robe, a girl with multiple piercings in Guatemalan print pants, and a guy in a dress shirt and slacks wearing a prayer shawl. But everyone else was just your regular college kid in jeans.

The passionate discussions, meanwhile, were anything but the norm.

"Religion is a pathetic crutch!" said Nat, the atheist.

"What do you believe in, then?" Tammy asked, perplexed. Earlier, she had invited me to the Catholic Student Association's spaghetti dinner.

"I think we all need to detach from our definitions of religion," said Cho. He was a Buddhist.

I was fascinated. I still felt like an outside observer, but I loved hearing what people believe at their deepest levels and why.

Our midterms were after the holiday break, so I only had a couple of weeks to get ready. Tilting back in my chair in my bedroom in New Jersey, I contemplated the stack of books in front of me. I picked up a thin paperback with a brown and black cover called *Honest to God.*

Within seconds, I was drawn in. The author was an English bishop named John A. T. Robinson who, while bedridden, took a hard look at his faith. Among other things, he questioned the expectation that people must instantly feel religious when the church bell rings. For him, the most authentic prayer was "waiting for the moment that drives us to our knees."[1]

As I read his words, I felt a warm "lightning flash" inside my head and chest—a simultaneous intellectual and emotional "aha." I'd always had trouble praying on demand and had just assumed I wasn't religious. But if I understood Robinson correctly, the sense of something beyond myself that I often felt in nature and while writing in my journal was in fact a form of connection to a Higher Power. I didn't have to follow the rules and dogma of any particular religion. I could pick out the teachings and rituals that resonated with me from different faiths and create some of my own, forging my own spiritual smorgasbord.

As this powerful realization sunk in, the colorful stripes on my childhood wallpaper started to blur and merge before my eyes. I no longer felt the desk and chair beneath me; I lost all awareness of my body. Soon, I completely dissolved—floating in a buzzing, limitless "electricity" that felt both like nothingness and all there is. Suddenly, a surge of warmth gushed in, and I was flooded with an incredible feeling of loving and of being loved and a deep understanding that I was connected to everything and everyone in the entire world. I stayed in this euphoric state until a chirping bird flew me back into my body at dawn.

I still didn't consider myself a religious person, but one thing was certain: That night, there was no denying the inexplicable connection I felt to something much bigger than myself, and that something felt like pure love. Spirituality was no longer something merely intellectual and outside of me. I now recognized it as the deepest part of my being.

A few weeks later, I chose my field of study: Comparative World Religions with a minor in Psychology.

"Comparative *what*?" my mom asked.

I laughed. I knew exactly what she felt.

"Why don't you major in computer science?"

"Ugh, banging on a keyboard all day and sitting in front of a screen? I'll go mad! Besides, what could be more important than learning what matters most to people on their most profound level?"

"Take at least one programming class."

"Forget it, Mom."

Senior year, I had to write a culminating paper encapsulating all four years of my college studies. It was due in a few weeks, and I was still struggling to choose a topic. I had read and discussed every major religious text, from the Bible to the Buddhist Sutras, and studied all the foremost schools of psychology—Skinner, Freud, Jung, Maslow, and more—how could I put it all together into a thesis-length paper, focused around a single question?

I thought about my two favorite religious scholars, Wilfred Cantwell Smith and Mahatma Gandhi. Smith was a renowned religious historian who pioneered the comparative study of religions. He discouraged the "we're right, you're wrong" attitude and instead advocated the "pluralist" view that all world religions are equally valid. Gandhi took it one step further and wrote, "Just as a tree has many branches but one root, similarly, the various religions are the leaves and branches of the same tree."[2]

I was intrigued, yet confused. Were all religions leading to the same, shared "truth," or was everyone walking toward different, but equal, truths? Did it matter?

That was it! I had to go find Smith, a comparative religion scholar who had taught at Harvard. I'd heard he was still alive and living in Toronto. My burning question was this: Did he, like Gandhi, believe that all world religions lead to the same ultimate truth?

Four days later, I was in his home. His wife Muriel welcomed me in, serving me tea and straightening the red and blue crocheted Afghan on her husband's lap. Professor Smith was a kindly white-haired man with glasses, who spoke softly and thoughtfully while rocking in his mahogany chair. We talked for over three hours. By the end of our conversation, he confirmed that he did believe that all world religions were variations of the same ultimate reality. I thanked him profusely for his wisdom and hospitality.

After listening to the interview tape, I realized I was still missing the psychology part of my thesis. Psychology provided a broader understanding of why people think and behave the way they do, but how did that fit into this spiritual question of ultimate truth?

I went to Widener Library, hoping to find something helpful. Wandering down a narrow aisle in the stacks, my backpack bumped into a shelf, drawing my eye to a book by Viktor Frankl, *Man's Search for Meaning*.

I sat down in the nearest carrel and read it cover to cover. Frankl was a Viennese psychiatrist who survived the Holocaust. While enduring unspeakable hardships in Nazi concentration camps, he observed that his fellow prisoners who felt they no longer had a purpose were the first ones to die. He concluded that the main motivation we're all driven by is the desire to find meaning in our lives. Based on this insight, he created a new form of psychotherapy called "logotherapy" ("meaning" therapy).

I'd found my missing link. While Smith had demonstrated that we all share a common religious history and affirmed that we are all spiritually connected, he never really explained what that spiritual connection was. Frankl's theory identified that connection, namely that we all share a universal search for meaning.

Combining Wilfred Cantwell Smith's religious pluralism with Viktor Frankl's logotherapy, I wrote my senior thesis on people's search for purpose, in their own lives and in life in general. I concluded:

Whether we are all seeking the same, shared Truth or whether there are many different truths, we'll never know. What we share is the process—the existential search—as well as the goal of understanding life's essential meaning. Since we'll never attain our goal, the best we can do is to respect one another's attempts. If we focused less on our differences and more on the shared nature of our fundamental search, there would be a lot more tolerance and understanding in the world.

I laughed as I printed the last page and ran to go turn it in. I had gone to one of the preppiest, most academically esteemed universities in America and emerged a hippie.

Back in college, finding my life's meaning had felt like a daunting task—like we have to take some big leap to live our big purpose. When most people hear "go big or go home," they choose to go home. Working on John's sheep farm helped me realize that small steps toward living your passion are just as good as a big leap, so long as my contribution to the world is somehow useful. If all I accomplished was to make three more batches of shortbread to keep John and his farm going for another day, then I had done my part.

Are You Talking to *Me*?
Push Past Your Fear

Before coming to John's farm, I'd met an Indian woman at Mount Cook, in the Southern Alps of New Zealand. Looking out of the youth hostel kitchen window at the snow falling thick and hard, I noticed a woman who looked to be about sixty-five struggling with one of the largest suitcases I'd ever seen. I ran outside in my slippers to help.

Have you ever liked someone from the moment you met, without knowing why? That's how it was with Kamla and me. Although we had nothing in common culturally or generationally, we immediately connected and chatted for several hours over a pot of hot tea.

Before she left, Kamla handed me a tiny piece of paper with her address and phone number written on it. Too bad she didn't live in Thailand or somewhere else that I really wanted to visit. There was no way I was ever going to India. I had no desire to go to a country that destitute, crowded, and intense.

Three months later, I booked myself a one-way ticket to New Delhi. I had just gotten back to John's place from a mini-vacation in the South Pacific where I'd listened, spellbound, to riveting tales of India and other exotic lands from returning travelers. Ever since, I lay awake at night, my veins pulsing with excitement as I thought about all of the places I hadn't yet seen.

I left a phone message for Kamla, letting her know I was heading her way. As soon as I hung up, a cocky American guy who came to work on John's farm started telling me horror stories about traveling in India. "You know, they drug your water and steal your bags over there. I have a friend whose money belt was taken right out of her pants while she was sleeping on a train. Another friend was in a crowded market, when a guy pretended to bump into him from behind. Before he knew it, the guy had slit his backpack with a razorblade and stolen his stuff right out of it. Then there's the 'drop the baby' trick, where a mother will pretend to drop her baby, and when you try to catch it, she grabs your daypack and runs. You're going to have to watch yourself and your stuff every minute that you're there."

Now I was terrified about backpacking through India alone, especially as a single woman. I began having vivid nightmares about each of the scenarios he described. I bought a piece of metal mosquito screen, lining my backpack with it so I could hear a razorblade scraping metal on metal if someone tried to rob me. I also bought an extra money pouch, one for inside my pants and one to be hidden elsewhere. Even with these precautions, I was filled with anxiety.

My fear always shows up right on time, just before I have to do something risky or important. The conversation goes something like this:

Fear: "You know you really shouldn't do this. Something bad is going to happen."

Me: "Yeah, so you keep saying."

Fear: "No, this time I mean it. Don't do it; you'll regret it, maybe forever."

Me: "You could be right. Now, if you'll just step aside, I have something I need to do. I'm sure I'll see you again soon."

Sure enough, Fear is always waiting for me the next time, right where I left it.

But as scared as I was, nothing was going to stop me from seeing the world.

Leveling with Each Other
No One's Purpose Is Greater Than Anyone Else's

Kamla received my phone message twenty minutes before my plane was due to arrive in New Delhi. She and her husband didn't own a car, so she scrambled to borrow one from a neighbor and rushed to the airport.

Joining the hordes of people in the arrivals lobby, I was bombarded with sensory overload. Women in colorful silk saris and men in designer business suits hurried past me, elbowing each other out of the way. The airport loudspeakers blared with flight departures in three different languages, two of which I'd never heard before. I hadn't gotten a call back from Kamla before I'd left, so I moved to Plan B. Scanning my travel guide for a cheap backpackers' hostel, I couldn't find an affordable one that didn't have warnings about bed bugs and theft.

"Laurie!" Kamla called out, grabbing my arm breathlessly from behind. "Oh thank goodness, here you are!"

I felt as relieved as she did. We gave each other a big hug.

In New Zealand, Kamla had worn sweaters and jeans, but here, she had on a long, loose tunic with narrow-cut pants, which the Indians call Kurta pyjamas. Her husband was wearing a white, linen kurta.

"My name is Dalbir, but everyone calls me Dolly, he said, extending his hand. "I hear you're another globetrotter like my wife. Do you like skydiving? Besides my grandchildren, that's my new hobby!"

A grandpa who jumped out of airplanes. I immediately liked him too.

"We'd better go, ladies," he said, walking toward the baggage claim. "There will be more time for catching up once we get home."

I clung tightly to Kamla's purse strap as we pushed our way through the throngs out to the car.

The roads were just as crowded and chaotic as the airport. People honked, shouted, and shook their fists as we wove our way through roads packed with cars, bicycle rickshaws, two-seater motorcycle taxis, ox carts, cargo-laden elephants, people riding camels, and hump-backed cows wandering aimlessly wherever they pleased. A thick cloud of diesel filled my nostrils and lungs when I opened the window to let in some air. Although it was December, the weather was still sunny and spring-like.

Everything looked brown. The soil was brown; the dusty roads and sky were brown; the buildings were brown; even the people were brown. I found that color to be somehow grounding. Bouncing along in the back seat, listening to Dolly and Kamla chatting in Hindi, my fears about being in India disappeared.

Because Dolly was a retired army officer, the government gave his family a small house in a military compound twenty minutes from downtown. All of the buildings there were the same: square, cement block houses. The inside walls and floors were also made of cement, streaked white from being washed clean. The furnishings were simple, but tasteful—polished, carved wood with richly colored, sequined pillows on the couches and chairs. There were only two bedrooms, one for them and another for their two adult sons. I offered to sleep in my sleeping bag on their living room floor.

"No, no, no!" Kamla said, horrified. "Only servants sleep on the floor!"

"Absolutely not," Dolly said, "You'll sleep with Kamla and me."

I strongly preferred to sleep by myself on the floor, but they wouldn't hear of it. After protesting three more times, I finally had to give in.

For two months I shared a bed with the sixty-five-year-old Indian couple and their big, farting dog. I didn't mind sleeping with Dolly and Kamla so much, but that dog almost killed me.

⌢

Among the many things I learned while living with my Indian host family, I discovered that Indian fathers can be extremely protective of their daughters. Dolly, who called me "his American daughter," wouldn't even let me go downtown by myself for the first two weeks. When I told him that I soon wanted to explore other parts of India, he insisted on doing a test run, agreeing to let two servants drive Kamla and me on a day trip to the Taj Mahal.

As I stepped out of the car and approached the mammoth white structure, my mouth dropped open. For the first time in my travels, reality exceeded my expectations. The huge marble dome, with its towering minarets and mosaics of iridescent jewels, was even more impressive in person than it was in pictures.

"It's stunning!" I turned and said to the first servant, Chedi. He lowered his eyes politely to the ground.

"I mean really, I've never seen anything like it!" I exclaimed, stepping toward the other servant, Baghwan. He took a step backward so that he was again two steps behind me.

I couldn't get the hang of the Indian caste system. I was trying to respect the local culture, and I understand the history behind it, but I didn't feel comfortable treating anyone as less than equal. I never understood why certain groups were supposed to be "higher" or "lower" than others. It's not that I don't respect someone's accomplishments or position in life; I just don't believe there's a hierarchy of human worth.

When I interact with people, the only "level" I note is the depth of their communication. I've always viewed interpersonal interactions like a stereo equalizer. People are capable of relating on many different levels, from the most superficial to the most profound. Depending on my "relationship goal," I might choose to match their level or nudge them up or down the equalizer.

For example, if someone is just "shooting the breeze," and my goal is simply to connect in a fun, lighthearted way, I'll match his or her level and chitchat in return. However, sometimes I can sense that people want or need to be pushed to go a little deeper, such as when they're struggling with a relationship problem and can't articulate the real, underlying issue. Or sometimes I sense it's best to bump people up on the equalizer, like when they're getting stuck in fear or depression, and I can help lift them back up to a lighter, more hopeful place. Just as I adjust the bass and treble levels to maximize my music, I make adjustments up and down the communication equalizer to make the most of my interactions with people.

My Way, Not Your Highway
Find the Courage to Follow
Your Own Spiritual Path

"Taxi, lady?" "Rickshaw?" "Hotel?" "I love you, baby . . . green card?" As soon as I got off the train in Varanasi, I was swarmed by pushy hopefuls. Gripping my backpack tighter, my only thought was "I hope to God I don't get sick."

A few feet ahead of me, I saw a man pinch a female tourist on the butt. She was about five feet tall and looked like she weighed all of ninety pounds. She turned around and walloped the man behind her with an echoing slap. The man she hit looked completely shocked.

"Um, excuse me . . ." I said.

"What?" she snapped.

"You just hit the wrong guy."

"I don't care!" She stormed off down a side alley.

I was on the Ganges River at dawn. The smell of burning wood filled the air in the inky, chilly darkness. As the sun rose and my surroundings became clear, I realized that what I'd thought were pieces of driftwood were human body parts floating past the boat.

"Why are there . . . ?" Cutting me off, the oarsman pointed to shore.

Along the banks was row after row of thickly smoking funeral pyres where dead bodies were being ceremoniously burned.

In front of the pyres, thousands of people were wading in the river, washing their bodies and clothes and drinking the same water. I watched a man push a floating leg out of the way so he could continue to splash his hands in prayer. I was mesmerized and horrified at the same time.

⁓

I'll never eat chicken again. After being cooped up on a bus for two days straight surrounded by chickens in baskets and their high-pitched, non-stop squawking, it was enough to put me off poultry for life. I'd just come from Dharamsala, where the Dalai Lama lived. I had traveled all the way to northern India to meet the Dalai Lama in his hometown only to discover that he was back in mine, giving a talk in Boston.

I decided to make the most of it, and I ended up having a powerful experience at his monastery, listening to the monks chanting. Each baritone "OMMM" seemed to penetrate directly into my heart, swirling and reverberating inside my chest until the sound became part of my cells. When I left three hours later, I felt completely calm and at peace. If that stuff could be bottled, it'd put Xanax and Prozac right out of business.

After another twenty minutes on the chicken bus, I arrived in Rishikesh, a well-known Hindu religious hub. The Beatles had

studied there with their guru, the founder of Transcendental
Meditation. I chose a different ashram not too far away.

I knew several people who'd had life-changing experiences at
ashrams, and I hoped I would find enlightenment too. I decided to
stay for at least a month.

That spiritual venture lasted exactly three days. In the words of a
California Valley Girl: "OMG, *hated* it!"

From the stories I'd heard, I was expecting an environment of
joyful, ecstatic prayer within the fellowship of a friendly community.
Instead, the atmosphere at that place just felt oppressive. Nobody
greeted or interacted with one another; everyone was somberly
absorbed in their own prayers and tasks.

Once, I made the mistake of smiling and saying hello to a man
who was pulling weeds from the garden. He glowered at me.

I felt absolutely no union with something higher, just tension
and a sense of my own resistance to following someone else's rules.
We had to eat at a specific time, clean our dishes a certain way,
and pray in a designated manner with precisely dictated words. I
wasn't hungry for breakfast at 4:00 a.m. I didn't always feel moved
to pray using someone else's script. While I enjoyed some of the
communal chanting, I began to appreciate what Robinson had
written in *Honest to God* about being allowed to communicate with
your Higher Power on your own terms, on your own schedule, and
in your own way. I confirmed what I'd discovered in college: My
spirituality was an eclectic blend of various world religions and my
own unique practices and beliefs. Although the details were still
evolving, my path included not only flexibility and openness, but
also passion and connection with others, creativity and spontaneity,
love, humor, and joy.

I wrote in my journal on the third morning, "I find no God here,"
then I packed my bags and left.

It's Your Job
The Duty to Share Your Gifts

Buddhism? Check.

Hinduism? Check.

Judaism? Hmm, not really the best place for that.

Islam? I'll wait to check that out in Indonesia.

What was left on my list?

Ah, yes, Christianity.

What better place to get a deep taste of Christianity than in Calcutta (now known as Kolkata), former home of the famous Catholic missionary, Mother Teresa. I had heard that Calcutta was a place of intense poverty, and I was powerfully drawn to seeing the slums for myself.

For the fourteen-hour train ride to Calcutta, I could only afford the lowest-class ticket. I walked into the littered, dimly lit cabin crammed with people of all ages perched on ripped seats with their parcels piled high around them. The train reeked of perspiration and curry. Once I was lucky enough to find a seat, I didn't move. I had no companion to watch my stuff, and I trusted no one. I had witnessed enough petty thievery to know that if I even so much as turned my head, my belongings would be history. I popped an anti-diarrhea pill so I wouldn't have to use the bathroom.

Baksheesh, baksheesh!" ("Tip, tip!")

"You give me money, lady."

"Please, lady . . . p-l-e-a-s-e . . . "

All around me in Calcutta, people were crying, pleading, and moaning in an orchestra of suffering and despair.

A drooling blind man grabbed my pant leg and refused to let go. Filled with repulsion and guilt, I pried him off and kept walking. I had been raised with the Jewish ethic of *tzedaka*: "Always help those less fortunate than you." I sincerely wanted to hand him some money, but I had just given my last cash to a half-naked girl holding a wheezing, emaciated baby. There were so many needy people here; I couldn't possibly help them all. Who to relieve, and who to deny?

Perhaps I would find an answer at Mother Teresa's church. I kicked my way through piles of rotting garbage, ducked under corrugated cardboard and metal shanties, and wove my way through endless crowds of people and cars coughing out black gusts of smoke. Suppressing a gag, I hurried past an open pit overflowing with human waste. Everybody I passed seemed to be missing at least part of their eyes, arms, or legs.

"Is there such malnutrition here that people's bodies become twisted and malformed?" I asked a nun who was giving an armless beggar some water outside of the church.

"Many people maim themselves and their children, gouging out their eyes and mangling their limbs," she explained.

I was dumbfounded. "Why on earth would they do that?"

"It brings in more money."

I don't know how Mother Teresa did it. I felt nauseated my entire time there.

To this day, I try to give money to as many homeless people on the streets as I can. A recurring phrase keeps running through my head: *But by the grace of God go I.*

⌒

Calcutta made me realize what a luxury it is to ask such questions as "What's my purpose?" and "How can I best follow my passion?" Mother Teresa's purpose emerged in those slums. But what about the people she helped? What passion and purpose did they get to pursue? They were living on a subsistence level—literally hand to mouth. I felt more motivated than ever to find and pursue my purpose. If I was in any position to think about and figure out how I could best use my gifts and talents to serve, and if I could find the means to go do so, then I had absolutely no excuse not to. Finding the answer to how I could contribute to the world was more than a luxury; it was my *responsibility.*

Thou Must Chill!
Learn to Relax and Recharge

Creamy coconut milk melted into tangy lemongrass and salty, crunchy spring onion. "Mmmmm!" I cooed as the warm custard cup disappeared on my tongue.

"And for dessert," the woman said, handing me a clear plastic bag. I picked up a piece of sticky-sweet, perfectly ripe mango.

"Wow . . . whoa!" I exclaimed, surprised by the bite of freshly ground chili. She laughed with delight.

Everything in Bangkok was a magnificent feast for the senses. Whatever I touched, tasted, smelled, heard, and saw in Thailand screamed joyfully to every part of my body, "Wake up! You're alive!"

Before coming to Thailand, I'd trekked through the jagged, 26,000-foot peaks in Nepal, known as "the rooftop of the world." When hiking in Nepal, you don't camp; you sleep and eat in the local villages. My Australian trekking partner and I had underestimated how much money we would need. By the time I came staggering out of the Himalayas three weeks later—having lugged my heavy backpack at high altitude on only half a cup of lentils a day—my legs were trembling uncontrollably. I had a new appreciation for my body and how strong it could be.

I decided to spoil myself a little. Fancy salon haircut at the Bangkok Hilton: $15. Relaxing Thai massage: $8.50. Nice hotel room with clean, crisp sheets and a working fan: $10. Many of my friends had asked how I could afford to travel. I wondered how they could afford to live at home.

⌒

After a few days in Bangkok, I took a bus to northern Thailand. Riding an elephant wasn't on my bucket list, but it was a popular activity there, and it seemed like a fun thing to try. In the hill tribe village of Karen, as I clung to Jumbo's prickly neck, I listened to the two young women chatting on the elephant next to me. From their accents I guessed they were British.

"I don't think we should try opium, Catherine," the one riding in front said to her friend.

"I'm not saying we should, Marion; I was only curious what it does," said the one in back.

"I can barely stay on this elephant sober," I joked, hoping they wouldn't mind me joining their conversation.

They laughed.

We introduced ourselves. With her blue eyes, porcelain skin, and perfect features, Marion reminded me of my favorite childhood doll. Catherine was the more athletic type; lean and muscular with tousled sandy brown hair, she looked like she could compete in one of those "gigacathalons," where they run, swim, bike, and bake a cake upside down, all in under two hours.

After trekking with them all day, I discovered they were both highly intelligent women. They knew when to be flexible and easy-going and when to take action in a challenging situation. Best of all, they both had a fantastic sense of humor, and we spent hours cracking each other up. They were perfect travel companions, and we became inseparable for the next forty days.

Catherine and Marion shared my passion for the beach. I soon shared in their passion for coconut peanuts with Mekong and Coke.

Each evening, we watched the sun go down while sitting on our towels with our snacks spread out before us in the sand.

We explored Thailand's most scenic islands, including Ko Samui, Ko Pha-Ngan, Ko Tao, and Ko Phi Phi. Back then, many of the nicest Thai beaches were still undiscovered or just being developed. In Ko Tao, they literally finished putting the doors and windows on our bungalow when we arrived.

When we got to Long Beach on Ko Phi Phi, there were only seven tiny tourist huts in the whole place, and six were already full. It was getting to be nightfall, and there were no other options.

I told the girls, "If you keep my money belt inside with you, you can have the hut, and I'll sleep on the beach."

"Are you sure?" Cath asked. Marion was already half-asleep in the hut.

I picked a level spot on some powdery white sand near the edge of the ocean. Lying down on my sarong, I pulled my towel over me as a blanket. It was a starry, balmy night, with a tropical breeze blowing gently across my face.

I liked my new bedroom so much that I slept there for a week. Each evening, I'd lie down and close my eyes just as the first twinkling stars appeared in the night sky. Soothed by the crickets' lullaby, I would peacefully drift off to sleep.

Each morning, I'd wake up to the first rays of sunlight kissing my toes and the sound of the local fishermen getting ready to start their day. Wading into the still water while I had the ocean to myself, I'd take a morning dip before rousing my friends.

By this point, I was deeply tanned, and my hair was completely blonde, bleached from the salt and sun. I'm also convinced that my heart rate and blood pressure slowed down significantly. At times I felt so relaxed, I couldn't even be bothered to get out of my hammock to pee.

My Harvard friends wouldn't have recognized me if they could see me "just chilling." Catherine and Marion couldn't imagine me ever being driven. To the outside eye, I looked like your average beach bum. Internally, a profound shift was happening.

I was still in search of my purpose and of the purpose of life in general. But I realized now that I'd been hitting it too hard. If I were going to maintain stamina to pursue a larger meaning and mission, it was key for me to sometimes slow down and recharge.

My favorite place to unwind was the ocean. I would float for two to three hours at a time, oblivious to everything around me except the warm, nurturing water. For the first time in my life, I completely let go, relaxing every muscle, emptying my head and heart, listening only to the lapping waves. I couldn't tell where my body ended and the ocean began. I was one with everything, and everything was one with me.

By far the most stunning beach was our last stop, Phra Nang Bay. Long before the tourist industry, filmmakers, and rock climbers discovered it, we knew we'd found the jewel of Thailand. Sheer limestone pillars rose from the turquoise water while pearly, soft sand faded underfoot into the sea. When we weren't swimming or sunbathing, we explored the large cave on shore, climbing up steep walls on slippery ropes through its myriad passages. By now our group had expanded to a gang of seven, joined by Catherine and Marion's friend Paula, Cath's new Thai boyfriend Prin, a Danish guy named Henrik, and another Brit named Peter. At night, we ate fresh fish at one of the only three restaurants on the island, skinny-dipped after dark, and danced until the wee hours at a bar carved into the cave. Life was good.

Watching Prin and Catherine kiss, part of me hoped I too would fall in love during my travels. But I was also glad that I hadn't met anyone special, as I might have missed out on other relationships and travel experiences. Although I wouldn't have complained if Mr.

Right came paddling in on the next wooden boat, I was content with my flirty encounters along the trail.

I wish I could've stayed in Thailand forever, but my travel clock was ticking. I had only a couple of months left to get through Malaysia, Singapore, Indonesia, Bali, and Australia before showing up back in New Zealand to lead the summer exchange trip again. As I hugged Catherine and Marion good-bye, I already missed them. A special bond forms between backpacking buddies that's different from the friendships you make back home. Especially if you travel together for a long time, you go through things and see things that no one else can understand, no matter how many photos you show or how well you try to explain. Twenty years later, Cath and I still write, email, and talk on the phone. We're currently planning our next big trip.

⌒

At twenty-two, life was a wonderful adventure. I was drunk on the freedom of being able to go wherever I wanted, whenever I wanted. For fifteen months, I'd visited fascinating, off-the-beaten-track places, seeing things I never even knew existed. I'd experienced countries from the inside, as a member of the family. I'd interacted with dozens of diverse people and cultures, helping me understand new and different parts of myself.

I had embraced the world, and the world embraced me back.

3

"MAZEL TOV!" NOW WHAT?

When I was twelve years old, I got Bat Mitzvahed with my sister. "Mazel Tov! Welcome to adulthood!" everyone said, shaking my hand and kissing my cheeks. But after opening my presents and sending out thank-you notes, I was no more ready to be a grown-up than before I had memorized all of those Torah passages.

Now of legal age, I still didn't know how to be an adult. I had been back in the United States from my world trip for only three weeks. Unfortunately, my re-entry hadn't been as joyful as my travels. I arrived home just in time for a recession, penniless and without a job.

Many tribal cultures provide meaningful, practical rites of passage to assist adolescents in their transition to adulthood—things like sending them off into the woods with no food to learn how to hunt. In contrast, the focus of most Western coming-of-age ceremonies is a big party. We generally don't offer pragmatic instruction to prepare young people to become happy, well-functioning adults. My life question, "What do I want to do and be in the world?" now had practical constraints: "Can I do what I love and still afford to eat?"

One evening during my senior year in college, my roommates and I sat around our living room talking about what each of us would likely become in the future. "Becky, Heidi, Elise, and Ignacio are going to be lawyers . . . David and Paulie are doctors . . . Jason's an artist . . . Megan and Kevin are going to do something in business . . . and Laurie? Hmm. We have no idea."

Neither did I.

After four intensive years at an Ivy League school, I needed a break from academics, and I wasn't sure I'd ever go back to school. I certainly didn't want to go directly to graduate school, as had many of my friends. I wasn't going to become a doctor, go to law school, get an entry-level job in a Fortune 500 company, or do anything else that people were saying a Harvard graduate "should" do. I wasn't purposely rebelling; it's just that the current options felt so limiting, and none of them felt like "me." My interests and talents were much more diverse, something I first realized while hanging off a cliff in Switzerland.

Why Say "Or" When You Can Say "And"?
Appreciate and Allow Multiple Passions

My parents had promised I could travel every summer during college, and I held them to their word. Not only was I eager to visit my Swiss family and farm, but I also wanted to climb a serious alpine peak and learn German. Thinking it would be a great way to kill two birds with one stone, I had signed up for a *Bergsteigerschule* (mountaineering school) in the heart of the Swiss German Alps.

That was not one of my better brainstorms.

"*Diese?*" ("This one?") I called down to my guides, fifty feet below me.

"*Nein, nein!*" ("No, no!") they shouted back up.

I was trying to figure out which rope on my waist I should clip into the carabiner to secure me to the side of the cliff, versus the one that if released, would send me plummeting down the mountain.

My guides, Hans and Fritz (yes, those were actually their names) were about as good in English as I was in German, and they kept mixing up key words like "up" and "down"—very inconvenient when you're hanging off the sheer face of a rock.

As I dangled in my harness, I reflected on my visit that past week with my Swiss family. While I quickly fell back under the spell of my charming, homey village, I missed my Harvard roommates and friends, with their quick, witty senses of humor and passion for knowledge and the arts. I realized I was both a country mouse and a city mouse, a person who loved the relaxed, simple lifestyle on a farm and the exciting vibrancy of an intellectually and culturally rich town like Boston.

I've never understood cultures that push people to compartmentalize and specialize, criticizing anyone with multiple interests and skills as a "Jack of all trades, master of none." During the Renaissance, people admired masters like da Vinci and Michelangelo for their versatile passions and talents, recognizing that the ability to do many things competently is an advanced proficiency in and of itself.

In that moment, it dawned on me that it wasn't a choice of Switzerland or America, cows versus college; I could fit in many places and pursue multiple passions.

Now that I was entering the world as a young adult, I just had to figure out how to translate my multifaceted passions into finding a job.

Lean on Me

Count on Your Friends to See You through Life's Uncertainties

When I backpacked around the world, I loved having nothing tying me down. Now that same open-endedness made me feel unsettled.

"Why don't you come to San Francisco, and we'll move in somewhere?" said my college buddy David, who had a well-paying job at a bank.

"Can my college roommate Kevin join us too?" I asked. "He's always wanted to live in San Francisco."

"The more the merrier."

As soon as we arrived, Kevin and I started scouring the city while David was working, but the only places we could afford were in sketchy neighborhoods or had cockroaches scampering beneath our feet. Finally, we found a nice, split-level apartment in Pacific Heights, one of the safest, most upscale parts of town. The apartment was lovely, with hardwood floors, a sliding glass door leading out to a deck, and a carpeted upstairs area with bedrooms and a bathroom. The downside was that there were only two bedrooms, so we would have to take turns sleeping on a futon couch in the living room. Still, it was better than living in a roach motel. David secured the lease, and Kevin and I began our job hunt, as the days of diehard penny-pinching began. Kevin became the master of finding every $1 taco happy hour in the city, and I learned to make a package of noodle ramen last for three meals.

While my work and home situation were still less than ideal, my friendships with Kevin and David grew stronger. Living with two gay men was quite an education.

"Time to go to Safeway," Kevin would announce on Wednesday evenings. The Safeway grocery store in the Marina District was known for its unofficial singles scene, alternating between straight and gay nights, when dozens of the city's unattached folks would go to "shop."

"Why can't we ever go when it's straight singles night?" I asked.

"Sorry, Laur, you're outnumbered." David winked at Kevin.

One evening, as a compromise, we went grocery shopping on a non-singles night. I rolled my eyes as David put a second bag of frosted circus cookies into our cart.

"Those things are nasty; there's not a natural ingredient in them."

"Look who's talking, PMS girl." He was referring to the last time we'd gone shopping, when I'd insisted on buying Keebler's "magic middle" cookies, a disgustingly artificial chocolate chip cookie with frosting inside. I didn't just want those cookies that night; I *needed* them.

"Touché."

"Stop bickering you two, and pay attention; I'm about to teach you something," Kevin interrupted us. "Now, you see that cute guy over there?"

"Yes."

"Look in his cart."

"Why?"

Kevin pointed out, "Fresh pasta, fresh herbs, good bottle of wine." He smiled at David. "That guy's on our team."

"How about him?" I asked, pointing to an athletic guy with a baseball cap.

"Two six-packs of cheap beer and a frozen pizza. He's straight and single, but you don't want him."

"There's another guy buying fresh pasta." David tipped his head toward a well-dressed man halfway up the aisle.

"Take a closer look," Kevin said, "Cat food and tampons. He's either got a girlfriend, or he's married."

To this day, I can't help peeking into other people's grocery carts when I go shopping.

Of the four major life areas—work, home, health, and relationships—my first two were up in the air. And while I was generally healthy, I still wasn't happy with my body. But at least one part of my life was positive and solid: I had wonderful friends.

Be a Sexy Mama
Learn to Love Your Body

I struggled to make ends meet, working at various temp jobs whenever I could get them. I went on a few interviews: for a position at a social work organization providing assistance to the elderly, for an entry-level job in a bank's retirement division, and for a law firm as a legal clerk. But I was always told that I was either underexperienced or overqualified. Tired of eating ramen, I finally accepted a secretarial job at a major corporation.

Every day felt like Halloween as I donned my costume of a Brooks Brothers suit and abdomen-crushing pantyhose. I tried hard to fit in, answering the phone with my best saccharine greeting and cheerfully accepting every task I was asked to do.

My supervisor watched me like a hawk, eavesdropping on my phone calls and interrogating me every time I left my chair.

"Where are you going, Laurie?" she asked me accusingly.

"To the restroom, Shannon," I said, clenching my fists.

Thank goodness for Darlene and Rosy, the other two secretaries. I wouldn't have lasted one day in that place without them. Every morning, we met in the staff room for fifteen minutes before our shifts. Darlene and Rosy were both very large, middle-aged, African American women who were fond of coffee cake and other high-calorie snacks. One day, Rosy came in with two boxes of donuts, one to share and one for herself.

"My husband is worrying that I'm getting too heavy," she said.

"Oh no, that's ridiculous," Darlene and I lied, the way women friends do.

"You know what I said? I said 'Honey! The bigger I am . . . the more of me to love!'" She drawled the word "love" so it sounded like "luuuhv."

Darlene and I laughed. Rosy took another bite of her donut, grinning.

I walked to my workstation to begin my shift. "The bigger I am, the more of me to luuuhv!" I smiled, repeating Rosy's words to myself. Here was someone who was happy with herself, including with her body.

I had struggled with weight and body issues ever since grade school. I was a really chubby kid, and where I grew up, anything more than five pounds overweight was considered obese. The beauty icons back then were Twiggy and Cheryl Tiegs.

The playground bullies had a field day with me. "Hey fattie, wanna play four squares?" "What are you going to be for Halloween, a pumpkin?"

My mother was always concerned about the battle of the bulge, both in herself and her family. She kept up with all the latest fashion trends, but that stuff just didn't matter to me, at least not the way it did to my slender and stylish mother and sister. As a result, I got pegged as the ugly duckling of the family.

My mom decided to make me her personal makeover project. Shortly after I put on my first real bra at age thirteen, she announced, "You are going to need breast reduction surgery. I strongly suggest a nose job to go with it." I didn't do either, but when I was twelve pounds overweight in high school, she enrolled me in Weight Watchers. Soon, the whole family was in on it. Whenever my relatives came over for the holidays, they would comment on whether I looked thinner or heavier than the last time they'd seen me. By the time I was seventeen, what really needed making over was my self-esteem.

Once I left home, I became my own harshest critic. I felt fat and ugly most of the time. Trying to hide my big nose, I never let anyone take a picture of me in profile. Even though my bra size is average, I was convinced I had oversized boobs. It's a miracle I didn't develop an eating disorder. I certainly have great sympathy for young girls who do.

I wanted to like my body, just like Rosy. I joined a gym where a personal trainer told me to throw away my scale and focus instead on how I fit into my clothes and how much energy I had.

Of all the lifestyle factors I began changing—diet, exercise, sleep patterns—the most important was my attitude. Instead of looking at myself in the mirror and thinking, "God, I look horrible!" I tried to accept my body in whatever form it was presenting on any given day and made modifications that helped me feel better. When I was feeling bloated, I wore looser clothes. When I had bags under my eyes, I wore brighter colors. On a bad hair day, I put on a cute hat. I started eating healthier and avoided deprivation diets that I knew I wouldn't be able to sustain. When I didn't feel like doing my normal exercise routine, I gave myself permission to only do ten minutes on the treadmill. (Once I got to the gym, I usually ended up working out longer anyway.)

I also decided to adopt a more light-hearted attitude toward my body. On the days I felt worst, I'd wear playful jewelry and outfits that lifted my mood. I didn't beat myself up over having a little ice cream for dessert every night. I created a playlist of my favorite songs and rocked out on the Stairmaster like I was at a club.

As I continued having a kinder, more fun attitude toward my body, I discovered more parts of myself that I liked. I noticed how my baggy capris showed off my muscled calves, and how my "bad hair day" hat accentuated my light brown eyes. The prettier I felt, the more motivated I became to reach my health goals. My body responded in kind. I didn't feel good when I ate too much junk food or drank too much booze. I'd start to feel sluggish if I didn't move my body at least a little. In place of the negative childhood voices, I was now hearing my own voice, which was excited about the healthy, attractive me that was emerging. Within a few months, I dropped four sizes.

Twenty years later, I'm even more fit and down another size. I still struggle with my body image off and on, including my new nemesis of aging. I'm finding that loving my body is a process, as my appearance and health continue to change over time. But by maintaining that same attitude of self-acceptance and fun, the positive voice drowns out the critical one. I continue to make choices that keep me healthy; but even when I make bad choices, I don't beat myself up. I just get back on track as soon as I can.

I Quit!
Life's Too Short to Stay in a Crappy Job

Five months into my corporate job in downtown San Francisco, I couldn't take it anymore. After everyone else in my office had left, I took the elevator down to the lobby and crept into the middle of a cluster of eight-foot tall planters, the closest thing to nature I could find. I slumped onto the floor and leaned back against a potted palm. I'd been doing my best to be a "good" college grad, getting a job and always paying my rent. Looking down at my briefcase and perfect pumps, it all felt so vapid and meaningless. Suddenly, all of my frustration and unhappiness came tumbling out—*I hate these stupid clothes. I hate this stupid job. I hate sleeping on that stupid futon in the stupid living room.*

Apparently, everything in my life was "stupid." I'd reverted to the vocabulary of a six-year-old. I started to laugh, just a little at first, then uncontrollably. Then my laughter switched to sobbing. *What am I doing here? Is this really how I want to spend my life?* I buried my head in my hands and cried.

What other choice did I have? Between the American Puritan work ethic of "no pain, no gain" and my own family's unspoken lesson that you must struggle and work hard for success, I'd always been taught to "tough it out." Besides, I didn't want to let Rosy and Darlene down.

Trying to pull myself together, I thought about the last time I liked my life. I had been very happy in college a couple of years ago, and I always felt happy when I traveled. I couldn't re-enroll in college, but I could go back to exploring the world. In that moment, I knew what to do.

One month later, on Christmas Day, I left my modest belongings in a friend's closet and boarded a one-way flight to Mexico City.

Once I got there, my plan was to find a Spanish language school somewhere in Central or South America and a local family to live with while I studied. I'd learned from my travels that you always get better deals and have more options if you wait until you arrive and ask around, rather than booking ahead.

Armed with my entire savings of $5,000, a pocket-sized Spanish-English dictionary, and a small notepad and pen, I wasn't coming home until I could speak, read, and write Spanish like a native.

Hey Chica, It's for You
Find Your Calling and Answer It

I knew I had picked the right place the moment I pulled into Antigua's historic town square. It looked like something straight out of a travel guide:

> *Charming cobblestone streets wind their way past majestic cathedrals, alongside courtyards with bubbling fountains. A yellow stone arch frames the towering volcano that dominates the horizon. On weekends, the main square hums with the sound of playful marimbas, entertaining locals and visitors strolling through the flowering trees.*

Travel books usually make a place seem way nicer than it really is, but in this case, neither words nor photos could do Antigua justice.

As soon as I arrived, my Guatemalan host family took me in as one of their own.

"*¿Te gustan?*" ("Do you like them?") asked Ingrid, the eight-year-old niece. To welcome me, she was decorating the bright blue walls of my tiny bedroom with her newest crayon creations.

"*Sí, qué lindo*" ("Yes, how beautiful"), I said, helping her hang them up.

"*¡Eh, escucha esta!*" ("Hey, listen to this!") The teenage twins, Obed and Elisabeth, came bursting through the door with a dusty cassette player. Blasting their favorite song, they laughed as I tried singing along.

For each meal, my host mother, Tita, would go out of her way to cook my favorite foods. My host dad, Chicho, was a real ham and would do funny things like take my clean laundry off the line and dance around the kitchen with it draped over him like a toga. Every evening, the oldest brother, Samuel, would grade papers for his high school class at the desk in my room while I studied on the bed with the cat. I felt like a part of the family.

"*¡Eh, Gorda, ven aquí!*" ("Hey, Fattie, come here!") With all my weight issues growing up, I was horrified at first when my host family started calling me "Fattie." Fortunately, Samuel explained that in their culture, they describe people as the opposite of what they really are as a sign of affection. Tall people get nicknamed "Shorty," skinny people are called "Chubby," and so on. Still, it took some getting used to.

⌒

"*¡No, no . . . otra vez!*" ("No, no . . . try again!") My Spanish teacher Sergio, a brilliant and passionate man, accepted nothing less than my best. From day one, he spoke to me only in Spanish. Sitting at a small wooden table, he drilled me on grammar and vocabulary each day for hours, insisting I build my own textbook from scratch. After two weeks of my family immersion and one-on-one lessons with Sergio, I was conversational. Within two months, I was fluent, complete with a Guatemalan accent.

The Spanish language is not only beautiful, but it can also be very philosophical. For example, whenever you're describing a possible future event with the word *cuando* ("when"), as in "when I next go to the movies," you have to use a special form of grammar called the subjunctive. When I asked Sergio why I couldn't just use the regular future tense, he said, "Because the future is never certain."

In Latino culture, there are common phrases people say all the time, almost like mantras. One of my favorite is, "*Que le vaya bien*" ("May you go well"). Recognizing both that life is uncertain and that each life is a journey, Latin Americans make sure to wish each other well on their paths every time they part.

I also grew to appreciate the frequent question, "*¿Cómo puedo ayudarte?*" ("How can I help you?") Unlike in many other cultures, when Latinos offer their help, they actually mean it.

Another common expression is "*Mi casa es tu casa*" ("My house is your house"). Each time I heard it, I was struck by the warmth, trust, and generosity of a people who are continually willing to open their homes to others, including to those they've just met. Nobody is a stranger in their culture, unless he or she chooses to be.

Perhaps my favorite expression is "*Buen provecho!*" Usually said during mealtimes, its sense is "Enjoy! Embrace! Seize! Benefit!" expressing a strong desire for a person's enjoyment and welfare.

May you go well. May you help others in need. May you seize and enjoy life. May you not be a stranger, especially to those whom you love.

I was definitely learning a lot more than just a new language.

One afternoon a week I volunteered in Samuel's all-girls Catholic high school, teaching English to one of his classes.

"How you say again—day-teeng?" fourteen-year-old Angela asked me. Her friends giggled.

"Yes, dating," I nodded.

To motivate these girls to learn, I knew I'd have to keep it interesting. We played games and did role plays using practical vocabulary about things they cared about, which in their case seemed to be boys.

Apparently, it worked. Samuel said never before had his students made so much progress in learning English. The principal of the school noticed too and soon gave me my own class.

⌒

At age twenty-four, some considered me irresponsible. Others thought I was lucky. As I jogged through the foothills outside of Antigua, I could hear their voices in my head.

"When are you going to get a real job?" one of my parents' friends had asked at our last family Thanksgiving dinner.

"I wish I could've traveled when I was young," another sighed at the same meal.

I was still just trying to find where I belonged. By exploring the world, I was searching for my place in it. I wanted to contribute something valuable, to be of use. I just didn't know how, what, or where. Whatever I ended up doing, it would have to feel right. The last time I ignored my intuition and did what society said I was supposed to do, I ended up having a meltdown in the middle of a bunch of office plants. All I could do was to keep listening to my heart and have faith that when it was time, my path would become clear.

Just at that moment, as I jogged around the next bend of the dirt road, it hit me: "I love learning Spanish, and I love teaching English.

I love teaching and learning in general, and I seem to have a knack for both. I know what I want to be when I grow up!" As soon as I got home, I would apply to graduate programs in education.

Mr. Almost Isn't Mr. Right
Don't Settle for an Unfulfilling Relationship

"I have to see you again," wrote Matt, my former crush from San Francisco, in a letter that Chicho handed me one day at lunch.

I'd met Matt on a white water kayaking trip just a few months before coming to Central America. Intelligent, good-looking, and fun, he was like a young Sean Connery, complete with the sexy accent. We spent time together on various adventures around California, and I started to really like him, but he had a long-term girlfriend in England and gave no signs of wanting to break up with her.

I was surprised at how strong my feelings for Matt had become. We didn't know each other that well yet, and we hadn't even kissed; we were just flirting. Perhaps it was the tension of being just on the edge of romance that made me so attracted to him. When I decided to leave San Francisco, he tried to persuade me to stay, but it wasn't worth sticking around for a guy who was already taken. It took me a while to get over him, but by this point I had pretty much let him go.

Meanwhile, unbeknownst to me, Matt had broken up with his long-term girlfriend and decided to follow me to Central America. I never expected to hear from him again. Never in a million years did I imagine that he'd pursue me.

"I don't know what to do," I confided to my friend Jacki, who was visiting Antigua for a few weeks from Berkeley.

"Why not?"

"Well, I'm not sure I still have any feelings for him."

"There's only one way to find out, and that's by spending time with him."

"But I don't want to lead him on. I'd feel terrible if he came all the way down here, and I wasn't that into him."

"It's his decision to take a risk and come down here. The only way you'll know for sure is if you give it a chance."

"I guess. But something about it just doesn't feel right."

"Look, you really don't have anything to lose. You're here traveling anyway. If worse comes to worse, you can each go your separate ways."

"I suppose you're right."

My intuition was still saying no, but I let my head overrule it. Now that Matt was single, and I no longer had to suppress my attraction, perhaps my feelings for him would be even stronger.

I invited him to join me in Costa Rica three weeks later.

⌒

Matt grinned and waved excitedly as he ran toward me from the airport door in San José. As soon as I saw him, my heart sank.

Oh crap, wrong choice.

The sight of him didn't bring back the romantic attraction as I'd hoped it would. Instead, I instantly regretted asking him to come. Once again, my intuition screamed, "This is all wrong!" Once again, I overrode it. I heard Jacki's words echoing in my head, "You won't know for sure until you give it a try."

"Please God, let my feelings for Matt come back once we hit the road," I prayed silently, as I smiled and gave him a hug.

⌒

I'd met a guy in Guatemala who told me about a boat captain who took travelers into the Amazon jungle where only natives live. He supposedly hung out at the fisherman's market in Manaus, Brazil.

"Do you know Capitáo Pedro?" I asked a woman standing behind a vegetable cart. *"Ali"* ("over there"), she replied.

"Obrigado!" ("Thank you!") I said, using one of the three words I knew in Portuguese. I headed toward an older man with white hair who was smoking a cigarette on a broken crate.

Two hours later, we were motoring in his small wooden boat through thick, brown water. I felt like we were traveling down the melted chocolate river in *Charlie and the Chocolate Factory*. When we got to the intersection of the Amazon River and Rio Negro, I was shocked: The Amazon's murky brown water met the Negro's glassy blue-black water without mixing; there were two distinctly colored channels, as if there were an invisible barrier separating them. I wished I knew enough Portuguese to ask Capitáo Pedro how that was possible.

As we headed up the Rio Negro, the vegetation along the riverbanks became greener and denser. The water plants became gigantic; we saw lily pads as big as tabletops, some of them eight feet across.

"You want hold?" Capitáo Pedro asked me in his best English, pulling a snapping baby alligator out of the river and pushing it toward my lap.

I screamed and jumped backward in horror. Pedro laughed so hard he almost fell overboard.

Matt took it, holding it precariously close to his head.

"No finger inside water, please!" Pedro instructed, as he taught us how to fish for piranhas. Those things taste as tough as they look.

At the end of the first day, we stopped in a small village, which was really no more than a wooden building on stilts with a dock. A group of children came running out to greet us. They were carrying assorted jungle critters. One little boy extended a hairy, black tarantula toward me. Its body was as big as an adult man's fist, and its thick, twitching legs were as long as fingers.

"Ahh, no, that's very nice of you . . ." I said, slowly backing away, trying not to sprint back to our boat.

Another boy handed Matt a boa constrictor, which immediately wrapped itself around his lower arm in a firehose-sized coil. He grinned. I shuddered.

"This okay?" Pedro asked, handing me a three-toed sloth.

I didn't mind holding the sloth, not only because it looked dopey and sweet, but also because it was still half-asleep. I figured it'd be too tired to bite me.

As I was handing the sloth back to Pedro, a little girl put a baby howler monkey onto my shoulder.

"Seu nome é Pepe" ("His name is Pepe"), she told me. Pepe immediately walked down my arm and nestled into the crook of my elbow like he belonged there. Draping his tiny arm over my forearm and leaning his cute, fluffy head onto my bicep, he exhaled softly as he relaxed. I stroked his soft, furry back with my index finger.

"I thought you didn't like exotic pets," Matt teased, taking my picture.

After two days of being on the river, we arrived at Pedro's village, near Airão Velho. He took us to his home, a platform tree house that we could only enter by climbing up a rope ladder. His children were gorgeous; they had bright white smiles, glowing, healthy skin, and huge, brown eyes that looked at us with curiosity and delight. They clapped their hands and chatted excitedly when we arrived.

"They happy meet you," Pedro said.

For dinner, Pedro taught us how to tap sap from the trees with a sharpened stick and how to pound dried cassava root into flour. I was surprised and touched by how friendly, generous, and open Pedro and his family were toward us. Even though I was sleeping on a few loosely nailed boards high up in a tree, surrounded by poisonous snakes, scorpions, and who knows what other dangerous wildlife, rarely have I slept so soundly.

As we were heading back toward Otovalo in Ecuador, a kind-faced old woman with a long, white braid came running out of her house.

"¿*Quieren comer cuy?*" she asked.

"She wants to know if we'd like to eat some *cuy*," I translated for Matt.

"Sure, that'd be great!"

"Um, do you know what *cuy* is?"

She grabbed three guinea pigs out of a box and threw them, screeching, into a boiling pot of water. I thought I was going to be sick. After she removed their fur and insides, she started deep-frying them in a pan of hot oil.

By the time she served us our plates of deep-fried rodents, with their little legs sticking up in the air and mouths still wide open in a scream, I had lost my appetite completely. Matt, meanwhile, was extremely drunk on the homemade liquor she had served us and began ripping limbs off and gnawing on them with relish.

"Aren't you going to eat?" he asked.

I shook my head no and passed him my plate. Even inebriated, I just couldn't dismember and dip into sauce a little fella who looked exactly like my brother's favorite childhood pet.

On our way to Machu Picchu, we decided to stay and tour the city of Lima, Peru for a few days. We should have read the newspaper first.

Matt slept in while I decided to go visit the famous cathedral in the main square. At the beginning of the tour, the guide asked each of us to say our names and where we were from. When I introduced myself, he turned as white as a sheet.

"*¡Dios mío!*" ("My God!"), what are you doing here?" he asked. "Don't you know they hate Americans?"

"Who?" I asked naively.

"*El Sendero Luminoso*, the Shining Path. They're terrorizing the city and killing anyone who doesn't accept their Maoist Communist beliefs. Americans are in danger; you stand for everything they despise. Stay right behind me during the tour, then go back to your hotel and do not go out after dark." But Matt and I were going to meet in front of the Government Palace, where there was a midday changing of the guard.

As it got closer to noon, a crowd started forming that got steadily larger and larger. "Hmm, this must be a popular event to watch," I thought. Soon I realized that people weren't gathering to watch the guards. The group consolidated into an incensed, pulsing mass. The angry energy escalated as the mob began shouting, waving placards, and pumping their fists. Within a few minutes, a massive military water cannon came thundering into the square and started shooting thousands of tons of water into the crowd.

I was frozen to the spot, mesmerized.

"Let's get out of here!" Matt said, but I couldn't move.

"Right *now*, Laurie!" He grabbed the back of my backpack and dragged me out of the plaza, just as a spray of water hit my feet.

The cab ride to the airport was like driving through a CNN broadcast. A car bomb smoldered in the street to our right as we whizzed past burning buildings and angry people throwing bottles and rocks. I heard gunshots and shouting, almost as loud as the cursing of our driver as he sped us to safety.

⌒

The view on the Inca Trail to Machu Picchu was breathtaking. Green and blue peaks rose unexpectedly from brown, arid valleys. The climb was challenging, but our group hiked at a leisurely pace and took frequent breaks.

"Eww, look at your leg!" I said to Matt. While we were resting on a bench, he had placed his right foot into a clump of long grass. Where there used to be a white gym sock, his ankle was now black with ticks. I grabbed some duct tape out of my pack and tore off a big swathe, ripping off all the ticks in a single motion.

"Wow, you're brilliant!" Matt said.

"Let's keep moving and stay out of the grass. I wouldn't pat the pack mules anymore either." Given the looks of their mangy coats and spotted, bumpy legs, they were carrying more than just our food and gear.

"Everybody come look," called one of our guides on the fifth day, waving us over to the edge of a cliff.

I looked down and gasped. Below us was a massive monolith towering over a giant maze of rock walls nestled on a plateau. Machu Picchu was first discovered in 1911, but I felt like we were stumbling upon it for the very first time.

⌢

You learn a lot about whether you're romantically compatible with someone when you travel together. This is especially the case in second and third world countries, where you're often physically uncomfortable and away from all things familiar. On the road, I've seen both lasting relationships form and long-term couples break up, as people discover what their partners are truly like. I call it the "backpacking litmus test."

Matt and I were doing pretty well as travel companions, and my feelings for him were now mixed. Sometimes I felt strongly attracted and loved having him around; other times, I felt smothered and wanted to run far away.

Lying under Matt's arm one night, I was filled with conflicting emotions. What if there was something wrong with me? What if I was incapable of intimacy?

Deep down, my instinct was warning me to stay guarded because I didn't feel safe. I knew Matt cared for me, but I frequently felt judged.

After the first time we made love, I confided in him about something that made me feel vulnerable. After a long pause, he asked, "What other hang-ups do you have?"

As I listened to Matt snoring, my chest ached with the overwhelming sensation of being completely alone. I didn't regret my decision to give our relationship a try, but I just couldn't push away the gnawing, longing feeling that true love had to be better than this.

⌒

Six months after leaving San Francisco, I ran out of money. I realized this while searching for unique souvenirs at a Witchcraft Market in Bolivia.

"*Para la buena suerte*" ("for good luck"), said a stout woman in a black bowler hat and purple shawl who was selling all sorts of unusual items in glass jars. She opened a red cloth, revealing a shriveled llama fetus. For the special bargain price of twenty Bolivianos, she promised it would bring me eternal good fortune, but only if I buried it in the doorway of my house.

"*No gracias.*" ("No, thank you"). I didn't want a souvenir quite that unique.

"Are you going to buy something?" Matt asked, walking over to me.

"Nah, I'm out of cash."

"We can stop and exchange some travelers checks."

"No, I mean I'm completely out of money."

"I don't mind paying for both of us from here on out. It'd be fun to go to Chile and Argentina with you."

"Wow, that's a really generous offer," I said, "But I don't want to use up your travel funds."

What I really meant was, "I need to take a break from you." I wasn't ready to break up with him, but I needed some distance to make up my mind and heart.

"I guess we'll be separating when I start work in London in a couple of months anyway," he said, looking sad. "Looks like we'll be dating long-distance from here."

A long-distance relationship with Matt wasn't at all what I wanted. In my mind, our foundation was still pretty shaky. But I didn't want to hurt him.

"Let's just stay in touch this summer and take it from there," I said.

At the time, I occasionally withheld the full truth from people for fear of hurting their feelings. I thought it was the nicer thing to do. However, many times I would end up hurting someone even more in the long run than if I had just been honest from the get-go. I've since learned that both on the giving and receiving end of difficult news, it's better to be 100 percent truthful in the moment, even if it stings.

⁀

Matt and I met up again two months later at my parents' house in New Jersey.

"He's adorable!" my mom said to me soon after she met him.

"Ma, you're a sucker for any man who's good-looking and butters you up."

"Absolutely."

"Matt is great in a lot of ways, but there are some things between us that just don't work."

"You'd be making a big mistake to let him go. If you continue being this picky . . ."

"Laurie, can you help me take these bags to my car?" interrupted Janet, my mom's close friend who was also visiting that week.

I walked her out to the driveway and helped her into her car.

"Get in!" she ordered, opening the passenger door.

Confused, I obeyed.

"Now you listen to me, Laurie. I love your mother; I love her like a sister. But don't you let her pressure you into marrying the wrong man. I made that mistake with my first husband. He was handsome, intelligent, and charming too. My whole family pushed me into marrying him. I stuck it out for thirty years even after I realized I wasn't in love with him, for all the wrong reasons: social acceptance, the sake of the kids, fear of being alone and without money . . . all of it. I'm so thankful to have met and married Arthur, to finally have found true love at the age of sixty. If you don't love this man, no matter what anyone else says, cut him loose and keep looking. Wait for that someone special; you deserve it. You'll find your true love whenever you're supposed to. Now get out!"

She blew me a kiss and drove away.

I broke up with Matt that night.

There's No Place Like Home
Find Where You Want to Live

As my next big adventure, I embarked on a tour of the "most livable US cities," visiting Portland, Seattle, Boulder, Sun Valley, and Santa Fe, all of which were lovely. But as soon as I pulled into Berkeley, across the bay from San Francisco, I knew.

I'd been warned that Berkeley was a total hippie town. But once I was there, I learned and observed that since the sixties, Berkeley had become much more diverse. The atmosphere was friendly, open-minded, and relaxed. The people I talked to were smart, active, and engaged, but not neurotic or stressed out.

I stopped in a coffee shop on College Avenue. Two construction workers stood in line in front of me. Their boots and clothes were covered in dust, and one of them had his butt crack peeking out from the top of his jeans. They got to the counter, and butt-crack man ordered: "One double latte, hold the foam please, and a cappuccino with extra cinnamon, thank you so much."

Only in California.

Berkeley is foodie heaven. There are dozens of farmer's markets, bakeries, and cafes on every corner, stores filled with gourmet chocolate, cheese, and wine, and numerous five-star Zagat-rated restaurants.

As I walked up the residential streets from College Avenue toward the Claremont Resort, I marveled at the blooming gardens and the intoxicating scent of jasmine that filled the air. I hiked up a trail above the resort, stopping at a breathtaking view of San Francisco, the ocean, and the surrounding rolling hills. Here one could be a country mouse and a city mouse, all in the same location.

I wanted to shout from the hilltop, "Hi honey, I'm home!"

It's a tremendous feeling when you find your place—the spot in the world where you belong. I'd felt comfortable in many places before, but this was a much more profound feeling—the deep, calm recognition that I wanted to live here for the rest of my life. Some of my married friends have told me that they experienced the same thing when they found their life partner: the certain, matter-of-fact realization of "Yup, this is it."

In Your Head versus Almost Dead
Apparent versus Actual Danger

A few weeks later, I was living in a cozy shared house in Berkeley on a cul-de-sac near a park. Following through on my epiphany in Guatemala, I had applied to master's degree programs at a handful of graduate schools of education. While waiting to hear back, I worked several part-time jobs, including as a professional outdoor guide. I started off as a backpacking, rock-climbing, and backcountry ski instructor for UC Berkeley's wilderness program, Cal Adventures. Then I graduated to the "big league" in the wilderness world and was hired to be an instructor for Outward Bound. Outward Bound's mission is not only to teach people outdoor skills, but also to facilitate personal and social development. It was founded in the 1940s, and a lot of their gear seemed to come from back then. Neither tents nor Gore-Tex were allowed, only plastic tarps, metal frame backpacks, and yellow vinyl raingear.

While teaching in the wilderness, I observed that much of what holds people back is *apparent*, rather than *actual* danger. My job was to help people get past their perceived limits toward new realizations of what they were capable of, both physically and emotionally.

One of my first expeditions was a twenty-eight-day "classic" course in the Blue Mountains of North Carolina. My group would be completely cut off from civilization, getting our food resupplied by mule and specially adapted bicycle trailers. It was a "multi-element" class, including rock climbing, ropes course, and white water canoeing.

I set off with twelve eighteen to twenty-four year-olds and a veteran co-leader named Jake. Little did I know we were heading into a subtropical rainforest. It was over ninety degrees with 99 percent humidity that summer. The area was notorious for frequent, sudden lightning storms.

"Why are we learning CPR?" asked one of the students on the first day.

"Because most often it's the leaders who get struck by lightning, as they ensure that everyone in the group is all right," Jake responded. "So if we go down, one of you has to save us."

"Oh," she gulped.

"Now, let's run through the lightning drill again, assuming a kneeling position on our foam pads and packs. Remember not to let your hands or feet touch the ground."

We soon had a chance to do a lightning drill in real time. On day fourteen, we were on a steep granite cliff, doing a lesson on how to do multi-pitch climbs. It had been a beautiful, sunny day. Toward the late afternoon, we heard a loud "crack" as a clap of thunder exploded. The sky was rapidly darkening, and a bolt of lightning struck a nearby ridge.

"We've got to get down right now, Jake!" I shouted to where he was climbing with some students about fifty feet below me. He nodded and began descending quickly.

"Darcy, Al, I need you two to climb down to this rock ledge where I'm standing," I told the two students above me.

They both came crashing down at the same time, almost knocking each other over. Darcy panicked. "We're gonna die! I don't want to die!" She wailed and crisscrossed back and forth on the ledge, tangling her and Alan's ropes into a tighter knot, caught in a frantic May Pole dance.

"Crash!" another clap of thunder, then "flash!" Another lightning bolt, only this time right behind us.

"Darcy, stop moving; I've got to get you two down right away," I barked.

Thankfully, I managed to get them safely off the cliff, where we grabbed our backpacks and bolted into a low stand of trees 200 yards below. The rest of the group was already huddled on their sleeping pads in the shrubs. A sharp jolt of energy ran through the ground just as I leapt onto my pack and knelt on it for dear life. The hair on my arms was standing straight up, and my whole body was buzzing. Jake looked at me with fear, then relief. One more second, and they would've been using their CPR skills.

Two weeks later, I took a group of teenagers on a mountain rappel. As an instructor, I knew there was no way they would fall while lowering themselves down from the cliff—they were in a secure harness and tightly roped in. But from their perspective, having to take a blind step backward off a 100-foot precipice . . . they're convinced they're going to plunge to their deaths.

"I can't do it!" whimpered Benji, "I'm going to fall and be paralyzed for the rest of my life!"

He had been up there for about an hour.

"All you have to do is take that first step back; the rest is cake. Six times I've watched you almost do it, and six times you've given up. I know you can't see what's below the ledge, but you've got to trust the equipment to hold you. I checked your harness and knots twice; everything is all set. If you stop clinging to where you are now and just go for it, you'll make the move successfully."

"I don't believe you! I can't do it! I hate you!" he shouted.

I decided to switch tactics.

"You know what? You're right. You're not as tough as I thought. Maybe you should give someone else a turn."

Smiling to myself, I heard him grunt then scream with surprised delight.

"Oh my God, I did it!" he cried. "Look at me! I did it! I did it!"

I looked up at him and waved. If only more people would just leap off that ledge, letting go of where they're stuck even when they can't see where they're stepping next.

"That actually wasn't scary at all," he said. "It was kind of boring."

It's true that as soon as you take that first step and your foot lands safely on the rock a few inches below, you realize that it was all in your head, and that there was nothing to fear. Reality, as compared to apparent danger, is often quite anticlimactic.

4

Born Again in Boston

I got into all the graduate schools I'd applied to. I hated to leave Berkeley, but the Harvard Graduate School of Education made me an offer I couldn't refuse. They accepted me into an extremely flexible program called an "individualized master's degree." After describing what I wanted to learn and which resources they had to support my interests, they would let me create my own course of study. A do-it-yourself degree—perfect for me.

When I told my family about my decision, I got mixed responses. My sister and brother lived near the Harvard campus and were thrilled we'd get to spend more time together. My dad said, "It's great that you're going back to school, but why didn't you pick a *real* field of study?" Apparently, education didn't count from a doctor's perspective.

Growing up with a brain surgeon father was quite an experience. While other kids complained about having to listen to their parents' classical music, my siblings and I were subjected to hours of *Neurosurgery Today* tapes, learning how to remove gray matter. Whenever one of us got a splinter, Dad would put on his surgical bifocals to remove it, staring at us with big bug eyes through what looked like a couple of shot glasses stuck to each side of his nose. On Halloween, he'd carve our jack-o-lanterns with a scalpel, cutting out the jagged teeth as precisely as he would a tumor.

While I found most of his quirky brain stuff endearing, there were some things that freaked me out. For one, his tie rack was a real human backbone hanging on the back of his closet door. There was also the creepy skull with a sinister smirk that he kept on his study shelf. Whenever I walked in there, I was convinced the thing was staring at me and whispering my name. No wonder I didn't go into medicine.

One of my best childhood memories is when my dad repaired my favorite stuffed animal when I was three. In a fit of toddler's rage, my sister had ripped the ear off poor little Mousey. I was distraught. Gently, my dad picked it up and put it on "the operating table," sewing the ear back on with perfect sutures, donned in his surgical mask and full medical scrubs.

My mom had a different reaction to my graduate school news. "I'm just glad you'll be in the country for at least another year."

When I called my grandmother and uncle who lived in Boston, they put me on speakerphone.

"As soon as you get out here, I'll set you up with a nice, Jewish doctor," Grandma said.

"Maybe she doesn't want a Jewish doctor," Uncle Harris retorted in the background.

"Nonsense. Now listen, Laurie, as soon as you get settled in, we'll go next door to the hospital and find out if there are any eligible men."

"What are we going to do, Grandma, just walk up to the reception desk and ask them to announce, 'Single girl in the East Wing?'"

Harris guffawed.

I smiled. If I had to go back to the cold, snowy winters of Boston, at least I had people there.

I Love You . . . Good-bye
End Unhealthy Relationships Even
If It Breaks Your Heart

Why does this guy keep staring at me?

I was out to dinner at a Chinese restaurant with a few other leaders of the summer exchange program where I'd worked for years. We were all attending a staff orientation that week. As I was choosing my dish, I could feel someone's eyes burning through my menu from across the large, round table. I glanced up, locking eyes with the France trip leader, Philippe. We gazed at each other intensely for several seconds, then his eyes softened, and he smiled. I blushed and smiled back. No one had ever looked at me like that before. Not a word was spoken, but it was a powerful conversation.

There was something about him that intrigued me. Quiet, almost brooding, but in a very sexy way. It didn't hurt that he was gorgeous, with thick, black hair, piercing hazel eyes, and chiseled features.

On day three of the orientation, I had an extremely unpleasant conversation over lunch with the program director. Quite unexpectedly, he blasted me with several hurtful comments. Picking up my tray, I walked across the quad to dump my trash in the dining hall, then cut through the woods to the dirt road entrance. After checking that no one was around, I burst into tears.

A jeep pulled up, and the driver rolled down the window. "Do you like ice cream?" he asked. It was Philippe. It turns out he had watched the whole exchange from a distance. He hadn't heard what was said, but he could tell that I wasn't doing well.

"Um, yes," I said, wiping my eyes with my sleeve.

"Well then, get in!"

He took me to a lake, and we shared a pint of brownie ice cream while I told him what had happened. Philippe listened patiently as I talked. Between the chocolate and his caring support, I began to feel much better. I felt so comfortable with Philippe, like it was okay to tell him anything. From the way he was opening up to me, I guessed he felt the same way.

Needing to stretch my legs, I stood up to watch the sunset. Philippe rose and stood behind me, so close that my head almost touched his chest. The hair on the back of my neck stood up as his presence surrounded me. I wanted to lean back and be engulfed in his arms, but I didn't dare move. As if reading my thoughts, Philippe wrapped his arms around me and pulled me in close. I exhaled and relaxed into his strength.

~

After our day at the lake, Philippe and I were like old friends. We put our sleeping mats next to each other in the staff house, and we giggled and gabbed until the wee hours of each morning. I sensed there was mutual attraction, but neither of us was crossing that line.

When he dropped me off at the Boston airport a week later, I was still unsure of our status. I was about to lead the Journalism in Eastern Europe trip, and he was leaving for France the next day. He had insisted on seeing me off, driving hours out of his way, but then he didn't even hug me good-bye.

"Have a great summer, Laurie."

"Yeah, you too."

He took a step closer and touched my shoulder.

A wave of electricity passed between us.

"Last call," the airline attendant announced.

Philippe smiled and broke away.

Was this guy just toying with me, or what?

Thankfully I had more pressing things to worry about right then. I knew nothing about either Eastern Europe or journalism; I had been added to the leadership team because I was "good with kids."

I waved good-bye and hurried down the runway, boarding a plane to Prague with two brand new co-leaders and fourteen aspiring journalists in tow.

⌒

After our trips, Philippe and I reconnected back at the exchange program headquarters. "I heard about your big adventure," he said.

Toward the end of my time in the Ukraine, a potentially rabid dog lunged out of nowhere and took a big chunk out of my side. The Center for Disease Control gave me ten days to live, unless I got an injection. There was no way I was getting a shot over there. I had been inside the local hospitals, and let's just say that it didn't look like hygiene was their number one priority. Fortunately, we were scheduled to fly home exactly ten days later. I made it just in time.

I was so full of rabies vaccine and so exhausted from the ordeal, I couldn't lift my head off the pillow for two full days.

"Listen, since you're obviously in no condition to get yourself back to your parents' house, why don't I drive you there?" Philippe said. "I'm heading to my folks near Philly anyway."

That would save me from having to figure out a bus ticket from New England to New Jersey. I gratefully accepted.

Later I would joke with friends that I never got out of Philippe's car. He quit his job and moved to Cambridge into my graduate student apartment. This arrangement was only supposed to last for a few weeks until he found his own place. Six months later, he was rearranging my furniture.

We tend to assume that in intimate relationships between men and women, it's the women who are more comfortable expressing their feelings and have to coax them out of the men. In our case, the roles were reversed. Philippe taught me how to trust another person enough to reveal my deepest heart. The first time he said something that stung, I turned my back to him in bed.

"What are you feeling right now?" he asked, his tenderness knocking down the wall I'd put between us.

"I don't know," I mumbled, fighting back tears.

He cupped my face in his hands and rolled me back toward him. "Please don't pull away from me. Just tell me what's going on."

When I opened up to him, he never judged or mocked me; he always listened attentively and lovingly, as I did to him. As a result, we had a fantastic sex life—the most powerful physical connection I had experienced to date.

One afternoon, I came back from class and found Philippe working at the desk. He'd had a terrible morning and started venting as soon as I walked in. As he gesticulated wildly, his unbuttoned shirt fell open. The top button of his jeans was undone. To emphasize a point, he laced his fingers behind his head and swung one leg up on the desk. *Nice boots*, I thought to myself.

"You're not even listening to me!" he said.

When he saw the look on my face, his angry mask turned into a sly grin. Without another word, he picked me up and carried me to the bed.

⌒

Six months into my new life in Boston, I couldn't imagine being happier. I was passionately engaged in my education career and equally passionate about Philippe.

A few days after Valentine's Day, I was in the middle of washing the dishes when Philippe made a shocking announcement.

"The love I feel for you belongs to Jesus Christ."

"I'm sorry?" I put down the dish and slowly sat down at the kitchen table.

"I shouldn't be loving a woman this much. I need to love Jesus first, then other humans."

I didn't understand what was happening. I felt my chest tighten.

"Why is it an either-or; can't you love both me and Jesus?"

"It doesn't work that way."

"Sure it can. There are lots of happy couples who are also devoted to their spirituality or religious faith." I searched for his heart through his eyes, but for the first time in our relationship, he looked away instead of looking back.

"That may be, but I need to devote myself to Jesus first."

I was stunned. We sat silently for several minutes.

"And we shouldn't have sex anymore."

I tried to mouth some words, but nothing came out. "So . . . what . . . what are you saying?" I finally managed to stutter.

"I either need to ask you to marry me, or I need to leave."

A few days later he moved out. I was devastated.

When I told my grad school buddies what had happened, they listened incredulously.

"Better this happened now than later," Holly said, trying to cheer me up.

"Sorry girl, but if a born-again is choosing between you and Jesus, Jesus wins every time," Carl shrugged.

"It wouldn't have worked out anyway. What were you going to do, convert?" Jen asked.

I looked down at the floor.

"You weren't going to convert, were you?" she repeated, sounding alarmed.

With tears welling up, I shook my head no.

As soon as Philippe left, I went numb to the core of my being. After having lived an adventurous, expansive lifestyle and experiencing one of the most emotionally, physically, and spiritually charged connections of my life, my heart now grew colder and darker than the vastest black hole in space.

At the end of each day, I plopped down on the couch in the apartment we used to share and just sat there for hours, staring into the distance. I shed no tears and felt no anger; there was only deafening silence. My heart didn't feel broken. It felt like it had been ripped out in its entirety.

But life goes on. I put on a "happy mask" and forced myself to move forward. With Philippe gone, I had more time for my studies. I finished my Master's with straight As and glowing recommendations from my professors. I landed three job offers and had the honor of delivering our class graduation speech. But on the inside, the sharp, dark pain continued.

⁓

One morning, as I was brushing my teeth, I got a strange gut feeling: *He's here.* I hadn't seen Philippe for several months. I assumed he had left town. But sure enough, when I arrived at the Education School a few hours later, his jeep was parked in front of the library.

For better or for worse, we still had an intense, psychic connection. It both thrilled me and caused me great pain. It felt as though we were on a lingering phone call, where the conversation was over, but neither of us was willing to hang up.

That night, he came to see me.

"I've been driving around the East coast for the past several months. New England is really beautiful country."

I nodded. "Where are you living now?"

"I found a great house with a bunch of guys just outside Cambridge owned by our church. You should come see it sometime."

From that point on, try as we might, Philippe and I couldn't stay away from each other. We continued hanging out off and on for the next few years. My college roommate Heidi teased me about how our relationship was dragging on, when we had only lived together for six months. "It's like a six-minute movie with three hours of credits!"

By continuing to be intimate, I wasn't moving forward, and he was failing to uphold his no-sex-before-marriage policy. Our lovemaking was as amazing as before . . . that is, until immediately afterward. Instead of cuddling with me like he used to, Philippe would beat himself up with remorse. His fundamentalist best friend called me his "Jezebel," blaming me for tempting him off his holy path. As a result, I would feel horrible too, like I was somehow a bad person for loving him.

Staying involved with Philippe was like being addicted to a drug. I constantly craved being near him, to feel him and to look into his eyes. By getting a "hit" of him every once in a while, I was preventing myself from making a clean break and going into full recovery.

When we used to live together, I would do the majority of the "logistical nurturing": cooking most of the dinners, putting special treats and cute little notes into his lunch bag, reviewing all of his resumes and job applications, and giving him a supportive ear during his many moments of stress. Nevertheless, the relationship had felt equal overall because he was giving to me in other ways— most importantly, teaching me how to be emotionally and physically intimate.

When we started spending time together again, I continued nurturing him with the same intensity, but the giving on his end tapered off. Soon our relationship became completely out of balance. In my twisted heart, I hoped that if I just gave him more and showed him how much I loved him, he'd want to come back, and everything would return to the way it had been. Instead, I ended up spending all of my energy loving a man who didn't ultimately want to be with me.

I felt I had to *do* things to be loved. I didn't yet realize that I could be valued and cherished just for being me. It certainly hadn't occurred to me that I could have a partner who adored spoiling me as much as I enjoyed giving to him.

The pay-off of over-giving is the "reward" of feeling needed. However, in return for my love and attention, I was punished by

Philippe's guilt and regret. I was learning a horrible, damaging lesson: Love equals pain. It would take me years to separate those two again and to recognize that love can be mutually nourishing and joyful.

Don't Show Me the Money!
Take a Risk and Trust that Money Will Come

A few days after graduation, I was weighing two job offers. Both were interesting, lucrative, full-time positions: working at a research firm in Berkeley investigating topical school reform issues and working with the founder of the charter school movement in Minneapolis to track the movement's growth nationwide. I knew that my passion was public school reform, but I didn't know which opportunity would provide the best way to get started on my career path.

That night, I awoke at 3:30 a.m. with an epiphany: "I have no business telling anyone how to improve the public school system if I haven't been in the trenches myself." I decided to gain experience by working in an inner-city Boston high school.

That afternoon, I turned down both job offers and called my parents.

"I've decided to volunteer in an inner-city high school," I told them happily.

"You've got student loan debts, and now you're going to work for free?" my mom asked in disbelief.

"You said no to the job offers?" my dad repeated, confused.

"I know it sounds crazy right now, but it feels like the only right thing to do."

"We're sorry, we don't have any teacher openings this coming year," Larry said. He and his co-principal, Linda, ran a cutting-edge high school for Boston's most underserved kids that had just been approved as one of Massachusetts' first charter schools.

"I am willing to volunteer."

"Why would you want to do that?"

I explained my late-night epiphany.

"Well, what can you teach?" Linda asked.

"I speak French, German, and Spanish; I've taught English as a Second Language, and I've coached teachers on how to do hands-on learning and community service learning." I added, "I also know quite a bit about charter schools."

"It'd be great to have a Spanish teacher, Larry."

"We'll see you in three months," he said, shaking my hand.

So there it was; I had my "job" for the fall. I had a modest balance remaining from my student loans, which I calculated could be stretched out for several more months. I'd survived on a shoestring budget for most of my adult life; I could eat ramen for another year. I especially liked the lime shrimp flavor.

Next stop, the Harvard School of Education. I thought I'd ask if they'd let me take classes toward my teacher certification while I'd be teaching full-time.

"We don't have an *a la carte* program just for certification," the head of the teaching program told me. "We only have a year-long Master's degree for teachers in training."

"I just got my Master's degree. Besides, it looks like I only need to take two more classes to fulfill the same requirements."

"There's just no precedent for it here; I'm sorry." He went back to the pile of papers on his desk.

I paused for a moment and said, "Sir, I'm going to be blunt. How many Harvard undergrads do you know who are willing to work for free as a teacher in inner-city Boston?"

He looked up at me over the top of his glasses, then smiled. "I'll talk to the admissions office and see what I can do."

Linda and Larry eventually found some grant money, and soon I was a full-paid teacher. It turned out that working in the trenches was precisely the right move to gain firsthand experience and to earn credibility with the people in the schools I was trying to help. This was now the third time that I'd left behind the security of job offers and a steady paycheck to pursue what would make my heart sing instead. All three times, I landed in a better place, doing something I liked more, making more money. Some people think I'm lucky; others say it's the Law of Attraction. All I know is it's just the way it seems to work. When you're being your authentic self, doing what you were meant to do, the money always comes. It may not come from where you expect or exactly when you want it, but come it does, often more abundantly than before.

It's Awesome, but It Ain't Always Easy
Live Your Passion Day to Day

My alarm buzzed at 5:30 a.m. As I sat up, a pile of mail slid off my chest. Rubbing my eyes, I realized I was still wearing my snow boots and winter coat. I vaguely remembered collecting the mail and climbing the three flights of stairs to my attic apartment the evening before. I thought I had just lain back on the bed for a minute.

I splashed my face, went downstairs, and hopped on the rusty 1967 Schwinn bicycle that I had gotten for free that summer at the end of a yard sale. "Only two gears work," the former owner warned me, "but you can take it if you want it."

Each morning, I pedaled that heavy bike up and down several hills across town to get to school. I taught for nine hours, then rode my bike back across the city to Harvard, where I was in teacher certification classes for another four hours. Once I got home, I'd stay up until 2:00 a.m. preparing for the next day at the high school and doing my certification program homework. After a few hours of sleep, I'd wake up and start all over again.

"Yo, Profe, whassup?" José asked, slamming down into his chair. I required each student in my class to pick a Spanish name. Many of them chose silly names like "Chihuahua" and "Taco," just to make everyone laugh each time I called on them.

"You're late, José, and you're not supposed to wear a hat inside. You know that—school rules."

"Yeah, but Profe, I'm serious, dawg, you don't wanna see what's under this hat."

"You know the drill, José; take it off."

José lifted off his knit cap to reveal the wildest, most out-of-control Afro I'd ever seen. The entire class cracked up. So did I.

"OK, you're right; please put it back on!" I waved my arm. Those kids made me laugh several times a day.

The neighborhoods where most of the students lived were the poorest in the city, filled with housing projects, drugs, and gang-related crime. Many of the kids were being raised by single mothers and never knew their fathers, who were either missing in action, in jail, or already dead. Sometimes grandparents took care of them, because their crack-addicted moms had enough trouble taking care of themselves.

Some of the kids tried to haze me at the beginning.

"What's a white lady gonna teach me about my own language?" Pablo sneered in Spanish, as he swaggered into my class on the first day. Fortunately for me, he had mixed up the past and present tense in his question.

"Well, for one thing, I'm going to teach you proper grammar," I quipped back, also in Spanish, correcting his mistake. "Have a seat."

One morning, Willie asked if he could be excused from my class to go to the bathroom. "I have to take a dump!" he announced to the whole class, holding his pants and jumping around dramatically. I knew he was planning to go smoke pot with his friend Jesús, but

I let him go. Four hours later, I ran into him and Jesús in the hallway.

"Wow, that's got to be the longest dump in history." I winked and walked by.

"No she didn't!" Jesús doubled over with laughter.

Willie never cut my class again.

With these kids it was all about respect. Respect is earned by respecting the other person; it's not something that's automatically given just because you're older or in a position of authority. By always giving the students the benefit of the doubt, they could see that I respected them, and in return, they respected me. I wasn't a pushover, however. As one of my students wrote on my evaluation: "Profe's real cool, but don't f*** with her!"

"Yo, yo, y'all!" said Jamal, poking his head into my classroom, stoned as a skunk. Jamal was one of the school's most notorious nomads, perpetually wandering the halls instead of going to class.

"Have a seat, Jamal, but if you're going to join my class, you have to pick a Spanish name.

"Y'all can call me El Rey (the King)," he grinned, pulling up a chair in back. Next came Guapa (Beautiful), El Jefe (the Boss), and several other class cutters over the following weeks.

In my classroom, my non-negotiable rules included:
1) Show up to class prepared and ready to learn.
2) No talking while others are talking.
3) No chewing gum or wearing headphones. (These two were all-school rules.)

I gave the kids three chances for each rule. For example, if they started interrupting each other or talking out of turn, I'd hold up my pointer finger, silently indicating, "That's one!" If they did it again, I'd hold up two fingers. Sometimes, the kids would test the boundary, pretending to open their mouths to say something again, while I started to put up my hand. I'd look at them with a glance that said, "Are you really going to go there?" then, laughing, they'd shut up. Soon, the students started self-policing each other: "Shut up, dawg; Profe's talking, yo!"

I believe that public speaking and presentation skills are just as important as academic skills, so I required each of my students to teach a lesson to the others. It didn't have to be on a serious topic; they could pick something cultural that was also fun, like Latin American food or dance. When it wasn't their turn up front, the other students participated on a peer review panel, giving the presenter feedback.

For his presentation, Jayshawn chose air pollution in Mexico City. He held up a colorful chart indicating that 80 percent of the city's air particles were contaminants.

"Where did you get that fact?" asked Yelitza, doing her job on the panel.

He blushed. "I just made it up."

Everyone laughed, including Jayshawn.

"I guess I gotta do it again, huh Profe?"

"I'll give you two points for honesty, but yes." I shook my head, laughing.

Next up was Jesse, who taught the class the history of his two favorite dances, salsa and merengue. After his presentation, he asked if it would be okay to turn on some salsa music and give everyone a dance lesson. I thought this was a great idea, not realizing just how sexy salsa can be. The kids were having a ball, gyrating their hips to the loud music. Suddenly, the door burst open. It was Ron, the Vice Principal in charge of discipline.

"What do you people think you're doing?" He hadn't yet noticed me standing in the corner.

"Jesse's teaching us how to salsa dance, Ron. Wanna join in?"

He looked at me, mouth agape. "Nope, carry on," he said, quickly closing the door.

Poor Ron. Last time he had stuck his head into my classroom, he'd seen one of the boys standing in front of the room with boxer shorts on his head and mismatched socks on his hands. In order to teach the kids colors, clothing vocabulary, parts of the body, and commands all at the same time, I had brought in several articles of clothing. Each student could pick someone to go up to the front of the room, then use the command form to instruct him or her what to do. Of course, they picked the most outlandish combinations possible to embarrass their friends: "Hold the blue sock under your nose." "Loop your right foot through the pink bra." Students who were previously getting Ds and Fs were now getting As and Bs in my class, and I wasn't an easy grader.

We always have energy to do what we love. Despite the stress, there was nowhere else I wanted to be. I loved those kids, and I sensed they felt the same affection for me. The exhaustion I felt was more than worth it.

You're the Right One for the Job
Trust You're Succeeding on Your Path, Especially When It Doesn't Feel Like It

"I can't take it anymore; there's just no point!" I slumped into a chair in Kay Merseth's office. Kay had been my favorite professor and mentor during my Master's degree program.

"I'm like the next generation of sheep, stepping up to be slaughtered! The public schools will never change. More and more kids will keep joining gangs, getting pregnant, and falling through the cracks. Why am I even trying?"

Life never looks good when you're exhausted. Overwhelmed, I burst into tears. She handed me some Kleenex and asked, "Can you think of at least one student you've helped?"

"I know where you're going with this, but that's not making me feel better. I can help a few kids, and you're right, that's important, but the whole system is broken. I'm pouring all of my efforts and energy into a sinking ship!"

At the end of my second year of teaching, my friend Jen asked, "Why don't you become a principal?"

"Yeah, right."

"I'm serious. Maybe you'll be able to make more widespread changes by being outside of the classroom."

"I'm only twenty-six!"

"So you'll be the youngest principal in Boston," she smiled.

After thinking about it some more, I realized it was a good idea. The head of the principal certification program at Harvard was even tougher to convince than the head of the teacher program had been, but once she saw how determined I was, she relented. I landed a job as an assistant principal at an innovative high school that was looking for a leader who was bilingual in Spanish and understood project-based learning. Once again, I'd be doing double-duty, working full-time while taking graduate school classes.

Although I was excited about becoming a principal, I was sad to leave my old school. Carmen, one of my students who had made huge emotional and academic improvements in my classes, wrote me a touching farewell letter (original spelling and grammar included):

Profe, you have been a teacher who many look up to and admire greatly. We have many good teachers here but Profe you one of the best teachers that we have. Loosing you will be like losing a special friend. Profe anything you do just don't forget the love that every one here got for you.

Her letter still hangs on the wall by my desk.

⌒

The students in my new school were more hardened. Most of them were gang kids, dropouts, and pregnant or parenting teenagers. Many of them were age eighteen and older, and several were there as an alternative to incarceration. The school was in a notoriously dangerous neighborhood, home base for the King Pins, a large Latino gang. Our school building was covered with graffiti, and there were bars on my office window. In the alley across the street from the school, shadowy figures sold drugs daily. Just to be safe, I tried to leave work before dark.

"Hey, Profe! You're a principal here?" Into my office walked J.D., one of my favorite students from the previous school.

"Yeah! It's great to see you again!" I said, giving him the "insider" knuckle-to-knuckle greeting.

J.D. excelled in his new environment, reading Homer's *Odyssey* on his own time for fun and picking out potential colleges. An intelligent, well-spoken kid of color with his grades was a hot commodity; he would probably get in anywhere he applied. I was excited for him; he had a bright future ahead.

But at the beginning of his senior year, his past caught up with him. Two years earlier, at the age of fifteen, he had been at a party and gotten into a fight. In an effort to save face in front of his "boys," he'd stabbed another kid in the arm. It had taken two years for the legal proceedings to be finalized, but now that they were, he immediately got hauled off to jail.

He looked so sad in his orange jumpsuit the day I went to go see him. I did my best to keep the conversation light, and I was careful not to mention the word "college."

When it was time to leave, the guard bent the rules and let me hug him good-bye. I walked slowly away from him down the hall.

"Profe!" he called out.

I turned around.

"Get me out of here!" he pleaded, as the guard dragged him back to his cell.

If only I could, J.D. If only I could.

I became a regular at the local jails and juvenile halls, visiting my kids, and I formed an unlikely friendship with a probation officer named Rex Mason. He was a striking, regal man, six-foot-two and muscular, a mix of African American and Cherokee blood. Having grown up in the streets of Boston, Rex was as savvy about the underbelly of society as I was naïve. Despite his cynicism, he had decided to give back by becoming a probation officer, hoping to help at least a few troubled kids make it out. He'd never gotten any public recognition for his service, and likely never would.

Rex and I were a good influence on each other. He taught me the ropes about all the kids' tricks, and I helped remind him why he had gone into this work in the first place. One day in my office, he said, "I don't get what you see in that kid, Manuel. He's bad news."

Manuel had been in and out of juvie halls since he was old enough to walk. I had decided to take him under my wing.

"Hola, I'm Laurie," I said to him, extending my right hand. He was slumped down in a chair opposite me with his hood pulled over his head and his arms crossed over his chest. He didn't move.

"So, I understand from your probation officer that you just got out this week."

He continued to glare at me without a word.

"It looks like you've picked your classes, so you should be all set there."

Silence.

"Well, I'm going to be checking in with you twice a week, just to see how things are going. I'll see you on Wednesday."

For the next two months, our interactions went pretty much the same, with me reaching out to him while he pretended I wasn't there. I cheerfully carried on the meetings as if he were keeping up his end of the conversation.

One day, he took off his hood before sitting down. He still didn't say anything, but I could tell by the way he was looking at me that he was starting to listen.

The breakthrough came at the end of the fall.

"Siento mucho que tu abuela este enferma" ("I'm very sorry that your grandmother is sick"), I told him. "I hope she feels better soon." Manuel was being raised by his abuela, whom he absolutely adored. I'd stopped by his house a few times to rouse his stoned butt out of

bed and get him to class, and I'd grown quite fond of the old lady myself.

One morning after the bell rang, I walked outside the front door of the school and asked the stragglers to come inside to class. One girl cursed at me under her breath as she dragged on her cigarette, refusing to move.

"You heard what she said, yo. Get it moving inside, girl!" Manuel commanded her.

She put out her cigarette and went inside. He held the door open for me and smiled.

Maybe Kay was right. Maybe it was enough to help just one kid move forward.

I'm Outta Here
Recognize When It's Time to Leave

As much as I loved my life, the long school hours and extended heartache over Philippe were taking their toll. I longed to return to California's sunshine and laid-back atmosphere, where I'd felt so at home. But leaving Boston would be hard. I had formed important networks in the Boston education scene, and I would miss my family and close friends.

Soon, events began to conspire to help push me out. I learned there was a chance my position at the high school wouldn't be funded again the following year. Three weeks later, my landlord gave me two months notice that he would be renting my apartment to his daughter.

While doors closed in Boston, new ones opened in California. I got a call from a colleague out there who wanted me to help him start the first charter school resource center in the country. Although it was in Sacramento, not Berkeley, it was an exciting opportunity.

"I'm going back to California," I told Philippe over the phone.

Dead silence.

"Can I see you before I leave?"

I still loved Philippe deeply. As painful as I knew it would be, I wanted to see him in person to say good-bye. We agreed to meet two nights before my flight.

"You're so beautiful." He nuzzled his face into the back of my hair and pulled me in closer.

"Thanks for always making me feel beautiful."

"You *are*."

If I stayed in his arms any longer, I would never leave. I gazed into his eyes one last time, then broke free and got dressed.

I felt a rock in the pit of my stomach as I watched him drive away. So many times during the past four years, I'd been left standing on the curb or peering through my window, aching with sadness at his departure and the anxiety of not knowing if and when he'd return. This time, I knew I would never see him again.

Although I didn't know it then, I had given Philippe a piece of myself, a piece that took me a very long time to get back. Years later, I found out that he drove straight to a monastery and checked himself in.

5

The Workaholic Turkey Farm

I arrived in Sacramento totally numb. Where once my fiery heart had been, there was now a frozen wasteland. Externally, I was happy to be back in California and to embark on a new professional endeavor. Internally, my spirit had shut down. It was just too painful to allow myself to feel and grieve the loss of everything I had left behind, especially Philippe. It was easier to just "check out."

A few days before Halloween, my business partner Charles and I arrived at my apartment with Chinese take-out and pumpkins in hand, ready to carve jack-o'-lanterns.

As we pulled up to the driveway, there were two police cars blocking our path. The front door was wide open, and the air conditioner was knocked halfway out of one of the side windows. An officer was carefully dusting the windowsill with black powder.

"What's going on?" I asked, dazed by the blaring walkie-talkies and whirling red lights.

"This can't be good," Charles said, getting out of the car.

Inside, my clothes were strewn everywhere. Drawers were half open, and my TV and stereo were gone. Strangely, so were all of my art supplies—a drawer full of magic markers, paste, and colored construction paper. The police told me a few days later that one of the thieves was a five-year-old boy. He was the one they'd squeezed in the window past the air conditioner to open the front door.

This break-in marked my third theft in only four weeks. That would teach me for trying to save on rent. I had moved into an apartment in an "up and coming" neighborhood right on the border of a decent area and a dangerous one.

The first theft had occurred three weeks earlier. On my first Friday of work, after riding my bike home, I'd discovered that the garage door clicker wasn't working. During the exactly thirty-two seconds it had taken me to go through the front door and open the garage door from inside, a white van pulled up, snatched my bicycle, and screeched away. My neighbor had witnessed the whole thing. Thankfully, I'd grabbed my panniers and brought them with me; otherwise, they would have gotten my wallet too.

The second incident occurred the following weekend, the day after I'd done my laundry. I had hung all of my clothes outside to dry, and when I went out to the backyard to collect them, the clothesline had been stripped. There was only one red sock left swinging pathetically in the breeze.

Three strikes and I was out. I gave notice to my apologetic landlord four days later after finding a cute little house for triple the rent in a much more upscale neighborhood.

"I'm so sorry about all of these thefts, Laur," my friend Terry said as we packed my things into the back of his pick-up. Everything fit into one load.

"Well, on the bright side, having most of my stuff stolen makes for an easy move."

While unpacking in my new house, I found my diary at the top of an open box. I opened it and stared down at the blank page in front of me. After a few minutes, I closed it again. For the first time in twenty years, I had nothing to write. Nothing joyful, nothing painful, not even anything neutral. I had neither feelings nor thoughts. There was only emptiness.

Workaholism Is a Real Addiction
Confront Why Your Life Is Out of Balance

Attempting to fill the void with work, my theme song became "I Haven't Got Time for the Pain." Charles and I had bitten off an enormous chunk, and we hit the ground running. We formed a resource center to help anyone interested in the charter school concept, bridging the gap between policymakers and oversight bodies on the one side and those who were starting and running the schools "on the ground." We made a great team: Charles had a background in policy, and I had school-based experience.

Starting a nonprofit from scratch is no easy task, especially when it's the first organization of its kind. All we had was a $130,000 grant, some handwritten ideas for workshops and publications, and a cutting-edge vision. Add to that all of the usual start-up tasks like choosing a logo, creating a website, developing office systems, and soliciting clients, and it's no surprise we found ourselves working around the clock.

"Should we grab some pizza?" Charles asked during our usual break time at 1:00 a.m.

"The pizza place just closed. The only restaurant still open is that all-night Vietnamese joint."

"Okay, let's grab a bowl of noodles and come back here afterward."

I don't know why I had bothered to get an apartment; I could've just kept a toothbrush at the office.

Our hard work paid off. Within six months, we had gained a reputation for in-depth knowledge and exceptional service, and our funding and client base increased dramatically. When our organization became internationally known, one thing was clear:

Charles and I hadn't just started a nonprofit; we were helping to pioneer a movement. And we quickly discovered that no matter how worthy the cause, most people just don't like change.

People have strong feelings about charter schools. Some working in public education hate and fear them, seeing them as unwanted competition. Those who aren't being served well by traditional public schools love them, regarding them with excitement and hope. Even those who have neither children nor employment in the education system often hold ardent opinions, based on their own school experience.

⌒

The clock beeped 4:00 a.m. Too foggy-headed to focus on the governance tool kit I was writing, I listened to my answering machine messages.

"Hey Laurie, it's Juanita from accounting. You know, leaving at 5:00 p.m. is not supposed to be a half day."

"Oh, hi Laurie; it's Ellen from the airport; I really enjoyed our lunch yesterday." You know you're traveling too much for work when the airline employees become your friends.

The next one was from Colin, my friend and colleague at the state Department of Education. Two days before, he'd left me a message: "Poor planning on your client's part does not constitute an emergency on yours." I'd left him a voicemail back: "True, but some of us don't have a cushy government job that mandates a fifteen-minute break every two hours." His new message:

"Maybe you should get one."

Listening to Colin's message, I had déjà vu.

"Okay, everyone, Christie is sick, so we'll need to cover her duties this week," the summer camp director told us at our weekly staff meeting. "We need someone to teach her beginning swimming class, cover the after-lunch swim, and be on nighttime duty in the girls' bunk."

"I'll do it," I said. Unfortunately, that meant I'd have no time off for the next ten days.

"Gobble, gobble!" said Sarah, a veteran counselor in her fifties. "Gobble, gobble!" she repeated. Sarah was legally blind and one of the wisest women I had ever met.

"What's your problem?" I asked, irritated.

"You're a turkey!" she mocked. "Welcome to the Workaholic Turkey Farm!"

"That's harsh. What does that even mean?"

"You complain about how tired you are and how much this camp asks of you, but you never say no. You just did it again—volunteering for everything and giving up your free time. If you're feeling stressed and overwhelmed, it's your own fault. You're like a turkey, running around with its head cut off, sacrificing itself for everyone else's Thanksgiving dinner. Gobble, gobble!" She walked away, flapping her wings like a turkey trying to take flight.

"How rude!" I thought, full of indignation. "How mean of her to blame me—somebody's got to do the work!"

As I sat at my desk in Sacramento, drained yet driven, Sarah's words finally sunk in. Back at camp, no one else had given up his or her free time. No one else taught an extra class or covered the night shift. Here I was as a professional adult, doing the same thing: working longer hours and taking on much more than I should. Why did I always jump in and put so much on my plate? Why didn't I ever set boundaries and say no? As I shut down my computer, I remembered a quote I had heard a hundred times: "On their death bed, nobody ever says they wish they had worked more."

I mulled over why I was such a workaholic. I was passionate about creating better schools for all kids, and I worked long hours to achieve what needed to be done. It didn't help that I was a perfectionist, holding myself to impossibly high standards. But why wasn't I equally committed to taking care of my own needs?

Part of it was family modeling. Both of my parents worked a ridiculous amount, my father as a surgeon and my mother juggling both her work and home tasks. I was clearly following in their footsteps. Moreover, others rewarded my hard work with admiration and appreciation, which felt great. At the core, though, was an old family dynamic; I was trying to get the attention and praise at work that I had always wanted from my dad as a girl. Combine all of those factors, and I had a recipe to keep me working way too hard for a very long time.

However, the workaholism was taking a toll. My mind and body were on constant hyper-drive. My muscles were cramped and tight. It was as if I were in continual "fight or flight" mode, poised to defend or sprint at a moment's notice.

My personality also began to change. I became irritable and critical. Things that wouldn't have bothered me began to frustrate me deeply. I started taking things personally and becoming defensive. When exhausted and under the gun, I sometimes snapped at people and had to go back and apologize.

I was disheartened. Just as I had questioned whether I was really helping the students in the classrooms of Boston, I was doubting whether I could truly make a difference on the state and national levels. Several years in the capital had made me very cynical about the way the world really worked.

"Does anyone making the laws actually give a shit about the kids?" I asked Charles wearily one late night over take-out. "It all seems to come down to money and power."

"Took you long enough to figure that out," he muttered. Charles was even more jaded than me.

Sarah had been right; working myself to death was my own fault, but I couldn't stop . . . I didn't want to. Deep down, I was afraid that if I stopped pushing myself, all of my repressed heartache and other locked-up feelings might come to the surface. I couldn't handle that right now. I still needed to coast, to stay frozen for a little while longer.

Change Is a Choice
Take Charge of Your Own Happiness

"Where have you been?" interrogated Dave, my first serious boyfriend in Sacramento.

"Working out like I told you."

He put his hand on my back. You're not even sweaty," he said. Where were you really?"

"I only did some light weights. What's going on, Dave?"

"What's his name? How long has this been going on?" he shouted, hurling a couch pillow.

"Whoa! You've got to calm down, *right now*!" He was like a two-year-old having a temper tantrum. "I'm not cheating on you. I went to the gym, just like I said."

"Prove it!"

"I'm going to go down to my car and get the rest of my stuff. If you haven't calmed down by the time I get back, I'm going home."

When I returned, he was in tears.

"Please forgive me," he sobbed.

"What happened?"

"My ex-wife and two of my last girlfriends cheated on me and didn't admit it until I busted them. When you were ten minutes late, I guess I just got triggered and projected all of that onto you."

During our eighteen months of dating, I spent hours counseling Dave through his tears and wrath. My college roommate Elise had a rebuff for men like him, "I am not your emotional gas station!" Truthfully, though, I didn't mind. Helping Dave work through his pain meant I didn't have to look at my own.

"Why do you keep choosing guys who are terrified of intimacy or look to you to heal them?" asked Jack, my close friend, one night on the phone.

"You told me years ago that you want a guy who's your equal. Why do you keep dating these guys who don't even come close?"

Other friends started referring to my boyfriends as my "projects."

"Why don't you forget dating and just have a few flings?" my friend Mike suggested. "Aren't your thirties supposed to be your sexual peak as a woman?"

Good Lord, if this was my sexual prime, how bad was the sex going to be when I got older?

Shortly after breaking up with Dave, I received a call from my old friend Mark.

"I really want to meet 'the One,'" I told him. "It's time for me, you know? But he just doesn't seem to be showing up."

"Well, unless he's the pizza delivery guy, I don't think he is going to just show up."

"What do you mean?"

"Laur, your lifestyle doesn't leave any room for you to meet and develop a relationship with someone new. An overworked woman with a packed schedule and bags under her eyes is not the most attractive offer out there."

The next afternoon, I approached Charles.

"When you asked me to help start this charter school resource center, we discussed the option of me living in Berkeley. I know we agreed that I'd start in Sacramento, but I'd like to move back there now. I think it's doable, with me working remotely and commuting as needed, but if not, I'm willing to leave this job."

"What's wrong with Sacramento?" he asked. "It's close to the mountains and has lots of great biking."

"I don't bike, and I never have time to go hiking or skiing. All I do is work here. A lot of my good friends live in the Bay Area. I need to start getting a life again."

He wasn't thrilled, but he agreed to try the new arrangement.

"Thanks, Charles."

Come hell or high water, this turkey was going to fly the coop.

6

Navigating the Keeper Hole

"Okay, everyone, this next drill can be dangerous, so pay attention."

As a way to reconnect with nature, I was training to become a white water rafting guide.

"You might want to put on a dry suit over your wetsuit; the water is still icy cold. All right, now one by one, we're each going to jump into that keeper hole."

"We're going to do *what?*" one of the other guides asked.

I knew how she felt. Each year, dozens of swimmers and boaters die in keeper holes, gasping for breath as they get dragged underwater, then pushed back up, then sucked down again by the powerful force of the raging water. This dude wanted us to purposely fling ourselves into a white water death trap. Seriously?

"Just remember how keeper holes work. The only way to get released is to dive for the bottom.

"The last thing you'll want to do after falling into a giant hole in the river and getting churned around is to head in the opposite direction of the oxygen source. But the river floor is where the main stream of current is located. Once you get into that flow, you'll quickly get pushed out of the hydraulic and spit up somewhere downstream."

"Laurie, you're up first."

Despite the terror I felt, I took a deep breath and dove in. Immediately, I was sucked in and cycled around and around in Mother Nature's giant washing machine. As I panted and thrashed, my muscles started to give way, and I needed my strength to get out. Against all of my instincts, I dove straight for the bottom. Sure enough, within a few seconds, I was bobbing like a cork a few yards away.

The only way out is to go all the way down.

After I got home from the white water training, I was exhausted to the bone. But I had two projects I promised to get on a client's desk by morning. Restless and not ready to jump into work, I wandered into my bedroom.

"I'm sick of working my ass off, chasing a never-ending 'to do' list," I suddenly snapped out loud.

"I *hate* that I still have dreams about Philippe." I kicked the bed in frustration.

"I'm so freakin' tired of being numb, numb, *numb!*" I repeated the word "numb" louder and louder until I was shouting.

After years of being frozen inside, a chunk of the iceberg had broken loose. I was mad as hell. And it felt better than feeling nothing at all.

Thanks, But That's Not Mine
Own Your Part, Nothing Less, Nothing More

My grandmother Mimi once told me that when I was three years old, all of the other little children used to follow me around the sandbox.

What happened to Laurie the Lionheart? I felt more like Laurie the Loser. Somewhere in my role as a nonprofit director, I had lost all confidence in myself as a leader.

My doubts got worse after a meeting I co-facilitated with Hal, another veteran charter school colleague. Hal was brilliant, and about the most arrogant person I'd ever met. He loved being in the spotlight, the "sage on the stage." He would brag about his professional exploits, telling the same stories over and over of his "ingenious" maneuvers and how he saved the day. He especially liked working with younger, less experienced colleagues, lecturing them ad nauseum while they sat taking notes in awe.

When Hal was presenting, he demanded everyone's rapt attention. Meanwhile, when it was my turn to present at the meeting, he opened up his laptop and started checking his email. When I was finished, he looked up and asked a question about something I had already addressed.

"As I mentioned earlier . . . "

"Don't repeat yourself! You're not making sense."

"I'm happy to clarify . . . "

"Stop rambling; you're completely incoherent!"

The people in the room looked uncomfortable, but said nothing. *Well, if you'd turn off your damn computer and listen, I wouldn't have to repeat myself, and my words might make more sense.* But I held my tongue. I didn't want to make a scene in front of everyone.

After the meeting, I asked to speak with him for a minute. I waited until everyone else had left, then closed the door.

"If you have a problem with my presentation, please speak to me in private. Do not disrespect me in front of a group again."

Hal rolled his eyes. "This is why women shouldn't be in a leadership position. You're too damn emotional."

"What are you talking about?"

"Everything that has gone wrong with this project has been your fault, and the people who've left this group have all left because of you."

I was shocked. "You're blaming me for all of our rough patches and turnover?"

"Everyone here hates you!"

"That's not fair . . . " I stopped as my voice cracked.

"And that's another thing, you can't take feedback," he scoffed, and walked out of the room.

⌒

"I must be a terrible leader," I confided to Robert, a good friend who was a veteran school administrator and former colleague from Boston. He was twenty years my senior with a heavy Boston accent. In a fatherly way, he called me "kiddo," and to tease him back, I'd call him "Bawby" (Boston-speak for "Bobby"). He had called to see how I was doing, so I confided in him about my recent experience with Hal.

"Well, kiddo, it's pretty obvious that Hal's intimidated by you. You went to Harvard; you're smart as hell, and you have skills and talents that he may never have."

"But he also has skills and talents I don't have. Our different strengths should make us a stronger team."

"You need to think more like a typical, competitive guy. When a man is out to win, and he thinks that someone could take away what he wants, especially power, he's going to do everything he can to knock that person down. That's the way it works."

"Oh great," I said. "I'm just trying to do a good job. I have no desire to go three rounds in the ring."

"It's not just men who operate this way. I have a hunch there are some women you work with who'd also like to see you go down."

"What did I do to them?"

"Nothing. They're either intimidated or envious or both. They make themselves feel better by badmouthing you. Women can be more vicious than men when competing for power."

"Why can't we all be successful at the same time?" My voice squeaked like a little girl's. I felt like I was back in middle school.

"You've got to stop being so naïve. Take off your blinders and start seeing the world and people the way they really are."

"Well . . . people suck."

"Welcome to the human race."

Now I didn't just want to quit my job. I wanted to quit the whole planet.

"So what can I do to get these people to like me and to support what I'm trying to do?"

"Stop worrying about being liked. Just *be* the leader. No matter what you say or do, not everyone is going to agree with your decisions or like your style. Knowing that, just make your best calls, stay true to yourself, and do the best job you can. That's all you can do."

"So, you're telling me to be more of a dictator?"

"Not necessarily. But when your team can't reach consensus, rather than trying to appease the strong personalities, stay empowered in your own authority. You can say something along the lines of, 'Thank you for your input; I'll take it under advisement. Sorry for those who disagree, but with the information I currently have, this is my best call at this time. I appreciate your understanding and cooperation.'"

"It's not that I'm afraid to take a stand and make a call that not everyone agrees with; I've done it quite a few times. What I hate is when people grumble and say mean things about me afterward."

Softening his voice, he said, "Not to sound too much like a shrink, but did you ever get yelled at as a kid?"

"Who didn't?"

"Can you think of a specific example when you got yelled at and you took it really hard?"

I flashed back to Disney World, into a loud, Wild West themed restaurant. I was eight years old, wearing a red and white checkered blouse and a cowboy hat. It was past my usual dinnertime, and I was hungry and eager for the food to arrive.

In the middle of the table was a basket of mini-pretzels. I reached forward and grabbed a handful of them. Still really hungry, I reached for a couple more.

"Don't be a piggy!" my father scolded, knocking the pretzels out of my hand.

I felt greedy and ashamed.

"Aren't you going to eat your dinner?" my sister asked when the meals arrived.

"I'm not hungry anymore," I mumbled, looking down at the floor.

"Yeah, I remember an incident," I told Robert. "What are you getting at?"

"Here's the thing. Just because someone is upset with you doesn't mean you've done anything wrong or that you're a bad person."

I felt a pang in my heart, and my eyes watered.

"Maybe you *should* be a shrink."

"Been where you are, kiddo. And while we're here, it also sounds like you take on more than your share of a conflict. Rather than owning just your part, you're allowing the other person to project all the blame onto you."

"But there are things I could do much better, Bobby, and I've made mistakes that I really regret."

"We can all do better, and making mistakes is the best way to learn. Just be sure that when you notice certain patterns of feedback, you make the necessary changes. Meanwhile, recognize that you're never going to be able to please everyone. Many people will ream you far more often and harshly than they'd ever look at what they need to improve in themselves. It's just much harder to look at one's own shortcomings than to point the finger at someone else's."

He continued, "There will always be people competing with you, disliking you, and judging you, especially when you stick your neck out there as a leader. It's the rare bird that gives a leader the benefit of the doubt and considers how hard it is to be in his or her position. You can't do anything about other people's hurtful thoughts or actions. All you can control is how you react. It's what you do with negativity that matters."

I wanted to crawl into a hole and never come out. Let someone else's neck get chopped off. While part of me heard loud and clear that I should just *be* the leader, the hurt little girl inside pouted, "I don't wanna!"

In my prior leadership positions, I'd felt grounded, loving, and clear. But in this job, I was so exhausted and stressed from the constant battles and never-ending workload that I felt like I lost my center. I didn't know who I was anymore, as a person or as a leader. As a result, I was taking on other people's negativity and operating from the same critical, untrusting place. That energy didn't really feel like "mine," but I'd lost my own compass and voice. Worst of all, I didn't know how to get them back again.

Robert had tried to cheer me up, but I was feeling worse than ever. I was in the "I suck" spiral. As anyone who's been there knows, it's not logical; it's not based in reality, and it ain't pretty. Before I knew it, I was bawling my eyes out, overwhelmed with the realization of how awful and unlovable of a person I really was.

For a moment, I wished I were still numb. This thawing process was excruciating. As the ice around my heart melted, my deeply repressed fears and pain were uncovered. I longed not to feel again, to just go through the motions of my day and "cope."

Then, it hit me: It was like being caught in the keeper hole. The only way to get unstuck from the churning was to dive all the way to the bottom.

⌒

"The land of fruits and nuts," my East coast relatives call California. While some poke fun, I discovered that these "fruits" and "nuts" truly understand personal growth. I was fortunate to have moved to California, home to many of the world's leading spiritual and psychological teachers.

I began investing large amounts of time and money on what I affectionately referred to as "working on my shit." Soon, I became a personal growth junkie.

I imagined sparring with Tom Cruise in *The Last Samurai* while I struck my fiercest warrior poses in yoga. Feeling like an overturned bug, I flapped my arms in the air in Pilates. I ingested only juice for two weeks to "cleanse" my system and "unblocked my chi" with acupuncture. I boiled up and gagged down funky-smelling herbal concoctions made from bits of trees, fungus, and other stuff scavenged from the forest floor. There was nothing I wasn't willing to try at least once—though I can't say I'll be drinking that nasty bark latte again anytime soon.

I read every spiritual growth book that called to me from the bookstore shelves, written by some of the wisest teachers both living and dead. I studied the Enneagram analysis of the nine basic personality types and consulted the I Ching, an ancient Chinese oracle that's still applicable to modern day living. I went to workshops on mystical subjects like Kabbalah and learned to mix homeopathic medicines. I started practicing Chi Kung and Buddhist meditation, learning about being still and centered in my mind and heart. I was a ravenous student.

We're All Psychic
Access Your Inner Knowledge

"Time for witchcraft class," Ollie said, tapping me on the shoulder in the dining hall. Ollie was my new friend from Germany. We were at Esalen, a retreat center in Big Sur, California, famous worldwide for its beautiful hot tubs on the cliffs overlooking the Pacific Ocean and its cutting-edge personal growth workshops. We had signed up for a class called "Psychic and Intuitive Healing."

Like Ollie, I had my doubts about the validity of intuitive readings. Coming from a conservative town, I hadn't had any exposure to alternative medicine or spiritual healers. My dad used to refer to chiropractors as "quacks."

"Reading energy is something that everyone can learn to do," said Shelley, our teacher. Shelley Hodgen was a down-to-earth, laid-back woman in her fifties . . . not at all what I had expected. When I enrolled in the class, I had pictured a flamboyant instructor with a colorful scarf around her head sitting in front of a crystal ball. The students in the class were also just "regular" people: lawyers, teachers, construction workers, accountants, and other professional types.

"Psychic abilities are not a special gift possessed only by a few," Shelley continued. "Intuition is something we all have and can learn to use adeptly with practice and an open mind. Developing your intuition is like going to the gym and developing your muscles. You may be weak and shaky at first, but the more you use it, the stronger it gets and the easier it is to draw upon. Very quickly, you'll be able to sense each other's energy."

While sensing energy sounded somewhat "out there," it also seemed familiar. We sense each other's energy all the time. Like when someone is pissed off, but tries not to show it, and you can sense that. My assistant came into work like that one day. She stayed behind her computer and didn't talk to any of us, but anyone who walked by her desk could tell she was seething.

It's not like we don't have experience accessing information outside our five senses and logical reasoning. Look at how popular dream analysis is. But for many, the idea of retrieving this kind of information during our waking hours seems more dubious and scary.

This psychic reading class wasn't the first time I'd learned about energy invisible to the naked eye. I first had that eye-opening realization during my sophomore year in college.

In order to graduate, each Harvard student was required to complete a "core curriculum" balanced among the sciences, humanities, and critical thinking skills. My roommate and I were looking for a painless way to satisfy our science requirement.

"Laur, I've found our easy science class!" Elise said. "Check this out, 'Space, Time, and Motion.'" She read the course description aloud: "'There will be no final exam or final paper, just an ungraded, three-page paper due each week.'"

"No final exam or paper? Let's do it!"

Little did we know we had signed up for the most intense science class of them all.

"Quantum physics? We just enrolled in a semester of quantum physics?" I shook my head in disbelief after our first day of class.

In the space of a few weeks, I changed from a science-phobic humanities major to a physics geek, as the study of matter and energy on the subatomic level radically shifted the way I perceived the world. I stayed up all night each time I wrote one of those ungraded papers, unpacking every mind-blowing concept:

When you watch a rolling ball, it appears to be a solid object that goes from point A to point B, but when you look under a microscope, it's just a bunch of atoms bouncing around and bumping into each other randomly. *Whoa!*

When we measure something on the quantum level, the measurements alter the very thing we're trying to observe. *No way!*

When scientists shoot electrons through two slits, the electrons can act both like concrete particles and waves. *Who needs drugs?*

As part of the course requirements, each of us had to teach a quantum physics lesson to the class. My teaching assignment was to compare physical laws on the macroscopic versus microscopic levels. I stood in front of the room and asked, "How many of you used to read the 'Dennis the Menace' cartoon? No matter how hard his mom tried to keep him under control, he just kept making a mess everywhere he went. That's 'entropy,' the second law of thermodynamics—everything tends toward disorder.

"Now imagine a bartender making a rum and coke. First he pours some clear Bacardi into the bottom of the glass, and then he pours brown coke on top. After a few minutes, according to the law of entropy, we would see the two layers taking on a uniform beige color as the molecules combine. Like with Dennis the Menace, the drink would progress from order to disorder, from two separate layers to intermingled molecules.

"Meanwhile, on the quantum level, the process is reversible; the drink could 'unmix' itself again over time. It's highly unlikely and might not happen for a million years, but it's scientifically possible. After a million years of sitting and 'unmixing' on a bar counter, the last swallow might pack a powerful punch!"

The class applauded as I sat down. "I'd like to see you after class," said Mark, the teaching assistant. *Uh-oh. Guess I wasn't "scientific" enough.*

Mark sat down in front of me. "I'm recommending to Professor Layzer that you become a teaching assistant for this course next year."

I was stunned. "I really don't think I'm qualified."

"I think you're just what we need."

Two weeks later, I nervously entered Professor Layzer's office. It smelled vaguely like yesterday's coffee. I was honored he had selected me for an interview, but I was feeling like an imposter. While I had thoroughly enjoyed his class, I was certainly no scientist. He, on the other hand, looked like the stereotype of a physicist, with wild, shining eyes and unkempt hair.

"Have a seat," he said, motioning to the wooden chair in front of his desk. "Tell me about your mathematics background."

This was starting off on the wrong foot.

"Well, sir, I haven't taken math since I had to in high school. I studied calculus and trigonometry and was in honors math classes and everything, but honestly, I haven't had much use for math since then."

He slowly scratched his chin. Perhaps I should have phrased that differently.

"How about science?"

"Um, I took Stephen Jay Gould's evolutionary biology class freshman year, and now I'm in your class." I blushed and looked down at the floor. "To be honest, I'm not really sure why I'm here."

"So," he asked, changing tacks, "Do you think science explains things or merely describes them?"

Now we were having my kind of conversation.

"In my opinion, Professor, it only describes. The scientific process is much like the study of religion. We are trying to understand our world, in this case with scientific tools instead of spiritual ones. But ultimately, we can never really understand the underlying cause for anything, be it the meaning of life or how the universe came into being."

He nodded and jotted something down on his notepad. We continued to talk for what seemed like hours. It no longer felt like an interview at all.

"Congratulations," he said, shaking my hand. "You begin fall semester."

I couldn't wait to see the look on Elise's face when I told her the news.

⌢

Since we know from science that our physical world consists of a bunch of microscopic particles bouncing around and intermingling in one large, collective energy field, why couldn't there be spiritual implications? Maybe intuitive readings are just another way of tapping into our interconnected energy field. Long before quantum physicists, our greatest spiritual teachers taught that separation is an illusion.

During the break Ollie said, "I don't think I have any intuitive abilities."

"Maybe it'd be easier if you call it 'gut instinct' instead; it's the same thing as intuition."

"Yeah, gut instinct," he said. "I like that better. I've always thought of intuition as something only women have; you know, 'female intuition' and all that."

"Whatever works, dude."

"Let's get back to work, everyone, and please pair up," Shelley said. "Each of us has an energy field around us. I'd like you to use your hands to see if you can sense any hot or cold spots around your partner's body."

As we practiced opening our intuition more, we eventually began to "see" colors and images in our mind's eye (much the same way that you "see" images when you dream), to sense feelings, and to "hear" words (again, like you do while dreaming).

Shelley explained that when "reading" others, we should use our intuition to share any information we might pick up. If we see an image or hear some words, we should first ask ourselves what it might mean. Secondly, we should check whether what we're sensing is the person's own energy or someone else's. "Energy from parents and former partners seems to especially 'stick' in other people's energetic space," she said.

"What's the difference between intuition and being empathetic?" one of the women in the class asked. "I mean, with strong empathy, you can feel what the other person is feeling. You can also relate to what someone else is thinking and feeling by drawing from your own experiences of when you've been through something similar."

That was a good question.

I partnered with a mid-Western man in his sixties who had been experiencing severe muscular pain in his right side for ten years. As soon as I started the reading, I "saw" in my mind's eye the image of a human fetus buried deep in the muscles of that side, then a pointing finger. I told him, "Whatever is causing your pain has something to do with a fetus and a finger pointing at you."

"Well, thanks for trying," he said and abruptly left the class.

At the next morning's session, he called me over and said, "Laurie, your reading was right on the mark. I know now what's causing my pain."

It turned out he had been involved in a car accident ten years earlier in which he had collided with a pregnant woman. She'd had a miscarriage, and blamed him for it. He had buried his guilt from this incident so deeply that it was still causing him physical pain a decade later.

Logically, I couldn't have known about this man's guilt after his car accident. I hadn't been present to witness the collision or the subsequent legal proceedings, and I hadn't been through anything similar in my own life. There's no way I could have used my empathy or my own experience to get to the root of his pain.

"I teach ongoing classes up in Mill Valley," Shelley told me at the end of class. "That's not too far from Berkeley, if you're interested."

I took her up on the offer and continued my training in intuitive readings and healings. Though I caught on quickly, I spent the first several months doubting and blocking my intuition. Still constrained by my mainstream upbringing, I feared people would judge me as a quack, so I saved them the trouble by judging myself instead. Over time, though, with enough support from my teachers and fellow students, I began to gain confidence in my new skills.

⌒

"Could you do a reading for me about my love life?" I asked Shelley one evening in class.

Two minutes into the reading, Shelley asked, "How much was your dad around while you were growing up?"

"Not very much. He was a brain surgeon."

"I see you as a little girl, trying to get his attention. You craved his affection and approval, but he was often too tired to even notice you."

I felt a lump rise in my throat.

"That's why you're attracting men who are emotionally unavailable."

"Your dad doesn't talk about his feelings very often, does he?"

"He's a great listener, but no, he doesn't really share his own feelings."

"That's why you're attracting men who want you to heal them. You're trying to help your dad open up. Ironically, you've adopted the same approaches as your dad, retreating into your analytic head as a coping mechanism. You especially try to avoid feelings like anger and shame. But underneath that detached, rational shield, you're actually a heart-driven, passionate person."

The lump in my throat made it difficult to swallow.

"In your relationships with men, you tend to lose your identity and put yourself second, trying to please and appease them. That's a pattern among the females on your mom's side of the family. Try to be more aware of when you're giving to men as a way to gain their approval."

I nodded, my eyes watering.

"In general, you often concede to others as a way to be liked or to avoid conflict. You're an easygoing person, and you get along well with many types of people. This chameleon-like adaptability has served you well. On the other hand, you often don't set strong enough boundaries and ask for what you need, want, and deserve. In energetic terms, you 'give away your power.'"

Man, it was the same things over and over again. Low self-esteem . . . not setting strong enough boundaries . . . not speaking up for my needs. At least I got points for consistency.

As Shelley spoke, she put her hand on my solar plexus, the energy center in between the belly and the chest that represents personal power. I felt a warm, pulsing sensation come through her hand.

"You especially give away your power in romantic relationships and at work," she said, shifting her hand to my heart.

"So, if I get into my heart more, stop worrying about being liked, and express my needs, I'll meet my true love?" I asked.

"Only if you want to."

"Of course I want to! I'm just afraid he doesn't exist."

"While you say you want to meet and marry someone who's your equal, you're energetically preventing yourself from attracting him. You're questioning whether you truly deserve to have someone who's on your level. The same with your views toward money and prosperity; deep down, you don't believe you deserve to have great wealth. You must shift toward believing that you deserve these things in order for them to show up in your life."

"So even if I really want certain things, if I don't believe deep down that I deserve them, they won't arrive?"

"That's right. When people don't get what they desire, it's often because they're sending out mixed energetic signals."

After Shelley's reading, I felt achingly alone. Clearly, I wasn't as ready as I thought.

One evening, as I was talking on the phone with my friend Shari, I suddenly "saw" an image of shining brown eyes and a bright white smile. I got a gut feeling that it was her brother who had committed suicide. I had never met him.

"Your brother, did he have brown eyes and a really bright smile?" I asked.

"Yeah, why?"

Then I "heard" a male voice say, "Tell her I really like the red circles."

"Um, he says he likes your red circles."

Silence on the other end of the phone.

"I'm painting red circles with my watercolor set right now!" she exclaimed, utterly stunned.

We weren't on our smart phones or computers with cameras; I had no way of seeing what she was doing. I had no idea that Shari even did art.

This energy reading stuff was really starting to get "out there." Biased by Hollywood and childhood ghost stories, I thought spirits were something to fear or something only crazy people imagined. How was I going to explain this to my friends and family, including my brain surgeon father? "Hey Dad, I hear dead people!" I could just see him dialing the psychiatrist.

But the more I talked with others about my experiences, the more I learned that it wasn't so unusual that I was connecting with the spirits of those who had passed. Many people whose parents or partners have died have told me that they could sometimes sense the spirit of that person around them. While there may be no tangible signs or evidence, they can "feel" their presence. The veil between this world and the next is indeed a lot thinner than we think.

Eventually, I started to feel more comfortable about the whole thing, realizing that spirits are just spirits, whether they're still in bodies or not. From that perspective, it was no stranger to receive information from the spirits of those who have passed than it was to read the spirit of a live person. Besides, who was I to let my fear of judgment get in the way? If my energetic sensibilities were expanding to include spirits who no longer had a body, then it was my responsibility to share the important messages that these spirits wanted to pass along to their loved ones.

Some of my friends were quite excited that I could communicate with the spirit world.

"Can you call in my Great Aunt Tessie?" one of them asked during her reading.

"It doesn't work like that. I can't just summon someone up like you order a pizza. I can send out an energetic request, and your aunt may come, but someone else might show up instead, or no one may respond at all."

"Oh," she said, a bit disappointed. Looks like I wasn't the only one who'd been watching too many Hollywood movies.

⌒

For the next several years, I spent almost all of my free time learning new healing skills. I became certified and trained in-depth in a veritable smorgasbord of Eastern and Western wellness techniques, ranging from the more mainstream to the wonderfully "woo woo." My mom proudly told everyone I was a massage therapist—I hadn't even told her about my talents in chakra cleaning or Shamanic soul retrieval.

"You've clearly been a healer in many past lives," Shelley said.

"Maybe," I said, not sure how I felt about past lives. I wasn't even comfortable with the word "healer." But I couldn't ignore the sensation that I had done all this before.

To Trust or Not to Trust?
When to Let People In and When to Keep Them Out

Because I was still working full-time at my charter school job, I was only offering my wellness services to friends and clients when I had time. Some would ask why I wasn't doing this work full-time. The answer was that I was still healing myself.

I had chronic pain and tightness in my shoulder and lower back that was so intense, I would spasm in my sleep. After getting a chiropractic adjustment, massage, or physical therapy, I would feel better for a little while, but the pain and tightness would return.

"So, do you let anyone in at all?" Marion asked. Marion Rosen was a world-famous healer who continued to work with people until a few days before her death at the age of ninety-seven. Through gentle touch and guiding questions, she was a master at helping her clients discover and release their physical and emotional pain. Her office was only a few minutes' walk from my house in Berkeley, so I had the honor of learning the Rosen Method directly from her.

"Yes, I let people in," I said, as my muscles stiffened, armoring myself against her soothing touch.

"And with men?" she asked.

Unexpectedly, I started to cry.

"I sense your trust issues began long before you started dating."

Trust issues? As I walked home, I pondered Marion's words.

My "trust barometer" was definitely off. I would trust the wrong people too quickly and get burned, then I wouldn't trust the right people for fear of getting hurt. The tension in my muscles was my body's way of forming a shell to protect me.

So how was I supposed to know when to open up and let down my guard and when to keep the protective walls up?

I thought about the times people broke my trust. In each case, the underlying causes seemed to be self-centeredness and jealousy. I had one former friend whom my gut told me not to trust, and for the longest time I didn't know why. It was only after I realized that she would consistently railroad over my boundaries to meet her own needs that my unease made sense. I don't think she even meant to break my trust; she was just completely focused on herself. Once I realized what was happening, and several conversations between us didn't resolve it, I had to respect myself enough to let our friendship go.

Whenever I felt an instant connection, be it with a man or a new friend, I'd be like, "Hey, I really like you, and we seem to 'get' one another . . . here, take my whole heart and please don't tromp all over it." I realized now that I should hold off a bit more, watching how that person interacted in different scenarios, especially under stress. By not opening up to new people too quickly, I could be more assured that my trust wasn't misplaced.

Trust wasn't all or nothing, though. True, there were some people whom I shouldn't trust at all, but those were in the minority, as were the people whom I could trust completely. Most people fell somewhere in-between: I could trust them up to a certain point, but not about all things and not at all times.

Even with this awareness, I could still get burned. The key was not to let my head or heart override my intuition. I'd learned too often that each time I ignored my gut, I only regretted it later. Ultimately, the most important person to learn to trust was myself.

Letting Go and Letting In
Accept Loss and Allow Yourself to Receive

"Stones have healing properties," explained the woman standing over me. "Each stone or crystal is unique. I'm going to place various crystals on different parts of your body. Does that sound all right?"

"Sounds good."

I was at a beautiful retreat center in southern Utah. I had signed up for a crystal healing without any idea of what it was.

She put on some relaxing music. As I drifted off, I noticed the lyrics were about death.

"Why did you play a death song?" I asked her when the music stopped.

"I sense that you have trouble letting go of loved ones, either those who've died or romantic relationships that didn't work out."

I nodded. "I loved someone several years ago, and I sensed he loved me too. I know that we don't belong together, but I just can't seem to get past my sadness of losing what we had. I'm afraid I'll never experience something like that again."

"Loss of love is a tough one. When you've shared a profound connection with someone, it's very hard to let it go."

As she spoke, she placed a large rose quartz crystal on my heart. I exhaled involuntarily, and my chest opened and relaxed.

"To quote Alfred Lord Tennyson: "Tis better to have loved and lost than never to have loved at all.'"

"Yes, but I don't feel that way right now."

"Even if you find a lifelong partner, most likely one of you will die first. Whether we allow ourselves to take the risk of love or whether we die without experiencing the joy of intimacy is our choice."

I thought about my grandfather, Poppop, who was devasated when Mimi died. They'd met when they were teenagers and were together for seventy years. As depressed as he was, at the funeral, all Poppop talked about were the good times and how grateful he was for having had her by his side.

"I do want to find love, but I just can't seem to let go and open up."

"You're going to have to work on letting yourself receive more in general. You must let others take care of you. In order to let others in, you'll have to allow yourself to be vulnerable again. Begin by experimenting with expressing your true feelings, even if you fear you'll be rejected or judged."

She placed a smooth blue stone on my throat. I felt a current of electricity run down my spine.

"After we're done, I want you to go out to the mountains and spend some time there by yourself. As you sit there, repeat these two mantras. First, 'I'm not alone.' In order for you to let go of lost love and open to future love, your spirit must remember that it is supported and surrounded by love at all times.

"Next, repeat, 'I can have it all.' You're allowed to have everything that you desire in your life; you don't have to settle for only some of those things. Do you understand?"

I nodded, trying not to dislodge the tiny crystals she had placed on my forehead.

As I meditated among the red rocks, I processed everything she had said. I put my head down on the warm, smooth rock and looked up at the puffy clouds.

Hey, there's a duck in a baseball cap, and over there is a frog on a flying carpet.

Suddenly I sat up. *Oh my God, Philippe is like these clouds!*

I'd been projecting onto him all of these wonderful qualities, just like I was projecting my imagination onto the clouds right now. Gentleness, passion, openness, and play . . . these were all qualities in *me*, and I could and would experience them in a romantic relationship again. By investing all my love in Philippe, I hadn't kept enough for myself. So when he left, it felt like all my love had gone with him. No wonder I didn't want to let him go.

I picked up a small white rock and kissed it. "Good-bye, Philippe," I said, and hurled it toward the cliffs.

Shadow Boxing
Make Friends with Your Dark Side

"Open! *Open*, goddammit!" Three weeks after returning from my spa retreat in Utah, I was screaming at a spaghetti sauce jar whose lid wouldn't budge. I started smashing it against the counter top in a rage.

I stopped in mid-swing. *Whoa, this isn't okay. I'm not okay. Where is all of this anger coming from?*

According to Jungian psychology, we all have an unconscious "shadow" side, which are those traits we're ashamed of and try to repress. Debbie Ford, author of *The Dark Side of the Light Chasers*, compares suppressing your shadow to holding a beach ball underwater; you'll soon lose your grip, and it will pop up somewhere else.

My dark side was rearing its ugly head, out of the blue and out of control. At this point, I was only yelling at inanimate objects, but I wasn't going to risk waiting any longer. I signed up for the next available course I could find on exploring my shadow.

"Write down all of the words you would hate to be called," the workshop presenter instructed.

Judgmental, arrogant, selfish . . . I could go on and on.

"Good. Now say, 'I am that.' These are the qualities you hate in yourself. You may openly exhibit them, or you may have spent your life trying to become the opposite. In either case, they are, in fact, part of your shadow."

We spent the next two hours in small groups, each taking turns claiming our dark sides:

"I'm an asshole," the first man said to our group.

"You're an asshole," we repeated back.

"I'm an asshole!" he said, more forcefully.

"You're an asshole!" we spat back.

"Shit, I *am* an asshole!" he laughed, and we all laughed with him.

The presenter then guided us toward seeing the gift in each of our shadow qualities.

"Let's start with 'selfish,' since I heard that come up a lot. When might it be good to be selfish? I'd like each of you to jot down your answer."

I thought about what the word selfish meant to me. I wrote, "Selfish = looking out for yourself first." I thought of the safety briefing on airplanes: "Please put on your own oxygen mask first before helping others." It makes sense; you can't help anyone else if you run out of air. That's exactly what I was trying to do these days by setting boundaries and taking more time for myself to relax and recharge.

It's amazing how the world can change when I reframe the way I look at things. There are positive and negative aspects to our shadow selves. There is no need to beat ourselves up in shame over having these traits. We just need to discern when our shadow qualities are operating in a constructive way, and when they are being unhelpful.

The Big Duh
Adjust Your Attitude

Two weeks later, my Harvard friend Suzanne came to visit me from New York. She had become a high-powered lawyer in a big, fancy firm. For most of our brief vacation, she had managed to control the urge to check her Blackberry, but now she made the mistake of sneaking a peek.

"Ugh, I'm so exhausted; I hardly got any sleep last night," she moaned. "I dread going back home today; it's going to be cold and miserable. And now, my boss wants me to . . . oh, never mind." She exhaled loudly and sat down on the bed. "I can't wait until I finally have enough energy again to do fun things without feeling so run-down all the time."

I bit my tongue. Sometimes, people don't want advice; they just need to vent. But something told me to speak up.

"Suzanne, you've always been great about putting my life in perspective when I've gotten off track. Would you mind if I shared a couple of thoughts?"

Looking nervous, she nodded.

"Sometimes we need close friends and family to point out the 'Big Duh.'"

"The Big Duh?" she chuckled.

"Yeah, something that's obvious to others but really hard for us to see. Like when everyone we're close to knows we're in the wrong relationship, but we're too mired in our emotions to realize it."

"I've been there."

"Well, in this case, your Big Duh is that you've got it backward. You keep saying that as soon as you feel energetic and healthy again, you'll do all of these great things that make you happy. But until you choose to be happy by leaving your stressful job and the city where you constantly feel cold and unwell, you're going to continue feeling run-down and bummed out."

I could see the wheels turning in Suzanne's head.

"Wow . . . it seems so obvious once you point it out," she said after a minute. "How do you figure this stuff out?"

"Trust me, I've been working on it."

After I spoke with Suzanne, I realized this period of my life hadn't been completely dark. I had plunged to the bottom of the keeper hole and come out safely downstream, stronger and clearer than before. I was primed and ready for a major transformation.

7

ALL ALONE IN
THE GREAT OUTDOORS

"Laurie?" Sparrow prompts me once again.

They are still waiting to hear why I've chosen to come on this vision quest. I feel like I've been sitting here for a lifetime.

Feeling everyone's gaze upon me, I exhale and begin. "The best way I can describe it is that I feel like I'm not fully being 'me.' I want to feel lighthearted, passionate, and happy again. I want to heal whatever I need to heal so I can meet my true love. I don't yet know what my bigger life purpose is, but I sense that I'm holding myself back from fulfilling it. In a nutshell, I feel like I'm squelching my own light."

Sparrow looks at me with understanding in his eyes. "Not being all you can be is like wearing the wrong size shoes. If you have a size ten soul but only wear a size six dream, eventually, it will become so painful, you can hardly walk."

As he goes on to explain in graphic detail the physiological reasons why it's important to clean out one's intestines before a fast, I review the itinerary:

Days 1–4: Start together as a group in a remote campground to prepare physically and emotionally for going into the desert alone.

Days 5–8: Spend four days and four nights alone in the Chama Wilderness, fasting and "seeking our visions."

Days 9–12: Come back together as a group to process the experience.

"What about using plants?" Bill asks.

"Plants?"

"Yeah, you know, uh, 'special' plants . . . "

"There will be no hallucinogens involved in this vision quest. The only thing you're to ingest is water."

Half of the group looks disappointed. The other half looks relieved.

"Trust me, you won't need any. What you're going to experience out there will be trippy enough."

All we're allowed for shelter is a plastic tarp, like the kind you see tied down on the back of a truck. Since we'll be in a sparsely vegetated desert, we may not have any trees or other anchor points on which to hang the thing. I wrestle with my big blue sheet of plastic, trying to figure out how to turn this flatbed cover into something I can call home. Just as I manage to prop it up with a tall branch and some heavy stones, Julie comes crashing through it, freaking out.

"This tarp thing doesn't even have sides! What happens if it rains? What if a wild animal comes and attacks me?" She wrings her hands and glares at her rumpled-up tarp.

"You'll be fine," I reassure her. I decide not to mention how fickle the weather can be in the high desert or the prevalence of scorpions and poisonous snakes.

"A vision quest is a rite of passage to honor adulthood transitions," Sparrow says, shifting to the spiritual aspect of a vision quest. "Many tribal cultures have rituals for major life changes, such as getting married, reaching a milestone age, and preparing for death. During these rites, the whole community shows their respect and lends their support."

What a contrast to our modern Western society. Our adult rites of passage are more like: Getting married? Here's a check. Just became a parent? Have some onesies. We gloss over just how much these major life changes can rock our worlds, and we often leave adults to get through significant transitions alone.

"Now, did you each ask a Council of Allies to hold vigil for you during your quest?" he asks.

I certainly didn't. The only people I know who hold "vigils" are either praying for an ill person who isn't getting better or mourning an untimely death—not at all the energy I want beamed my way while I'm out in some godforsaken patch of sand alone and without food. Instead, I simply asked my Council to "send me happy thoughts."

Next, we review the three stages of a vision quest:

- *Severance:* Leaving behind the comforts of home and letting go of the people, situations, and behaviors that limit us.
- *The Threshold*: While in the wilderness, "dying" to our former way of being and becoming "reborn" to the new.
- *Incorporation*: Bringing back what we learned on the quest to our community and integrating the lessons into our daily life.

"For each of these stages, there are powerful rituals you can perform to help you move through them," Sparrow says. "Write these down and bring the list with you."

On our last night at the campground, Sparrow looks around at each person in the group, then says knowingly, "Your spirit isn't drawn to go on a quest unless you're ready to make serious changes in how you're living your life. I've been doing this for many decades. Trust me, no one comes back from a vision quest the same person."

⌒

We arrive at our basecamp in the Chama Desert at 9:00 a.m. It's already baking hot. Our task for the day is to find the spot where we'll each spend the next four days and four nights alone, fasting and "crying out for a vision."

"When you think you've found your spot, ask the land for permission to stay," Sparrow instructs us.

Karen says out loud what we're all thinking. "What do you mean, 'ask' the land? You don't mean that literally?"

"In the same way you know when you want to leave or stay at a restaurant, you'll 'know' whether a spot feels right for you. Feel free to ask the question out loud, or just try to get a gut sense. As strange as it may sound now, you're going to be talking with nature quite a bit while you're out there."

He pulls out a map and shows us our options. "You can go up either of these canyons: Los Ojitos, which means 'Little Eyes,' or Cañada de las Fuertes, the 'Canyon of the Strong Women.'"

That's a no-brainer, I think to myself.

This canyon is "fuerte" all right; it's stunning. Eroding mesas expose their orange and pink striped underbellies, beckoning wayward hikers to the mouth of the canyon. Tempted by their siren call, I hike in a good forty-five minutes.

My heavy water jugs cut into my fingers, and my shoulders feel like they're being pulled out of their sockets. As part of today's recon mission, we're carrying half of our water supply to leave at our sites. I have no idea how I'm going to pack in the other four gallons, plus all of my gear tomorrow.

As I pause to rest, I see a light out of the corner of my eye. High to my left is a massive, sheer rock face glowing the same yellow-gold as the sun. In the foreground, like a silhouette, is a densely forested mountain saddle. "Absolutely gorgeous!" I breathe out loud, then pick up my water and keep walking. There's no way in hell I'm going to hike that far away and that high up with such a heavy load.

Fifteen minutes later, I stop dead in my tracks. To my right is a patch of soft pine needles on flat ground surrounded by a ring of trees that would make it easy to hang a tarp eight ways to Sunday. Ten yards away, there's a dry riverbed, which would channel the water safely in case of a flash flood. In front is a view of a lovely red cliff. If you called a Hollywood location scout and requested the ideal vision quest spot, this would be it.

"Hey, I'm going to check out this place," I call back to Annie, the only other one who's ventured this far back into the canyon.

She nods and keeps walking, leaving me alone.

Feeling a little sheepish, even though no one can hear me, I ask the land, "Can I stay?"

I half expect one of the trees to sweep me up in its branches like Treebeard with the hobbits in *The Lord of the Rings*.

Instead, I get more of a silent gut feeling. My gut sense is, *No.*

I'm surprised and a little hurt. "Can I please stay?" I ask again, hoping my politeness will be persuasive.

No.

"Can I visit?"

Silence.

My eyes tear up. The land is rejecting me.

Then I get another strong sense: *This isn't a rejection; it just isn't your place.*

Immediately, I know where my place is. I trudge back to the spot where I first saw the shining yellow rock. "That's a long uphill hike," I complain out loud.

Branches tear at my bare legs as I cross through three football-field lengths of sage, climb into and back out of a steep, dry ravine, then jump over a barbed-wire fence. I'm not even halfway there; I still need to climb two mountain ridges and hike up the side of the saddle to get to the cliffs. Snorting out of my nose like a tired work horse, I drop my water jugs, lash a tall stick to the fence so I can find my entry point when I return, and stuff a red bandana into my shorts pocket to mark my spot once I get to the top.

Smack.

"Ouch!"

Rip.

"Dammit!"

Crack.

"For crying out loud!"

Zigzagging my way up the ridge to the last steep pitch, I grab onto the underbrush to keep from slipping down the mountain as pebbles and dirt cascade in mini-avalanches under my feet. By the time I reach the top an hour and a half later, I'm covered in dirt, scratches, and bruises.

"Oh, thank *God*!" I exclaim. Then suddenly, I'm speechless. The view from this spot is so magnificent, I burst into tears. Below, a single trail leads through the painted valley as far back as the eye can see, winding through patches of sagebrush and sun-hardened soil. Waves of heat bounce off the rusty red landscape into the endless blue sky. The Golden Cliffs tower behind me like protective castle walls. With the sun now hitting them directly, the light on the yellow rock is almost blinding. I feel like Dorothy in *The Wizard of Oz* when they switch from black and white to Technicolor; the colors are so vibrant, they seem surreal.

I know this is my spot; I don't even need to ask. I pick up a stick and draw a line in the dirt in front of my feet. Mustering up my most official-sounding voice, I declare to the mountain, "I, Laurie Beth Gardner, leave behind anything that is preventing me from living fully." I already have a long list . . . and those are just the things I know about. I add, "And I release any unknown fears and ways I'm messed up that I'm not even aware of."

Before crossing the line, I continue in my Voice of Importance, "I now move toward shining as brightly as I can. I will have the courage and the clarity to come fully into my purpose, whatever that may be. Instead of getting stuck in struggle or heaviness, I will live joyously with lots of laughter and play." Stepping over the line, I plant each foot firmly on the other side and seal the deal: "I hereby cross into the threshold."

Let the games begin.

There's only one problem: There's nowhere to sleep up here. The saddle is an exposed ridge, about six feet across, dropping off sharply in all directions. The two knolls on either side of the saddle are equally steep and exposed. I'd have to get off this razor's edge and look for something lower down.

Have I hiked all the way up here for nothing?

I search for over an hour. Just as I begin to feel discouraged, I see a little patch of flat earth just big enough for my tarp. As I squeeze past a waist-high tree to take a look, a branch snags the red bandana from my pocket. A ring of small evergreens encircles the cozy sleeping spot. Nearby, a burnt tree that has nothing left but a few charred branches and a twisted trunk stands guard like a sentinel. Ahead is a magnificent view of the canyon below, and to my back are the Golden Cliffs. I walk to where the bandana is dangling from the branch, marking the spot. "I'll be back tomorrow," I smile.

Lose the Schtick
Unleash Your Inner Freak and Be Your Authentic Self

I sit down next to a cedar tree that's half dead and half alive, a metaphor for the "death and rebirth" experience of a vision quest. It's silent up here. From the cliffs behind me to the ridges below, there's not a single sound. I'm guessing it's around noon; the sun is directly overhead.

As I admire the view, my thoughts begin to wander.

Is it Father *Sun or* Mother *Sun? Why are vessels female, as in, "She's a good ol' ship?" I feel like my Subaru is more of a he. And what's up with Germans referring to objects not only as male or female, but also as neutral?*

So much for peace and quiet; my mind-chatter is deafening.

A friend once asked me, "How can you tell which voice is your real inner wisdom versus your ego or whatever it's called? I have so many voices in my head that it's hard to tell them apart."

I thought about my own experience and did my best to describe it.

"Well, for starters, I listen to what's being said. If it's anything fearful, negative, or judgmental, that's my ego. Inner wisdom is never mean or scared. I also notice how it's being said. My ego voice hops around from topic to topic—what the Buddhists call "monkey mind"—or else it stays on the same subject obsessively, telling me the same 'poor me' story again and again. Meanwhile, the voice that comes to me after I still my mind and emotions is always succinct, centered, and clear. It rarely repeats itself, nor does it need to. The best way I can describe my true inner voice is 'the wisdom that comes from my deepest place of knowing.'"

After sitting and gazing out over the canyon for a while, my head and heart finally quiet down. Away from the ringing of cell phones, endless stream of email messages, and other chaos of everyday life, I begin to experience stillness. Eventually, I hear only the sound of my own breathing.

Now seems like a good time to try talking to nature like Sparrow suggested. I turn and face the cedar tree next to me. Now how does one go about talking to a tree? It can't be any different than talking to my houseplants, I suppose, except that I've never expected them to answer back.

I sit very still and wait, I'm not exactly sure what for.

"Is there anything you'd like to tell me?" I ask.

After a few seconds, I get this reply: *You need to let out your wild side.*

Whether it's the tree's spirit or my own inner voice, I can't tell. To be honest, I don't really care. I'm open to listening to whatever I need to hear, from wherever it may come.

"My wild side? I think I'm pretty wild already—do you know all of the crazy traveling and outdoor stuff I've done?"

Not 'wild' in the sense of adventurous or 'back to nature'—that you've already discovered. I mean let out your inner freak. Dancing around your living room in your underwear doesn't count. You've got to let out your inner freak more in public.

"My inner freak?"

Where I grew up "freak" was considered an insult.

Everyone is a freak, Laurie, it responds, as if reading my thoughts. *You need to overcome your judgment and learn to cut loose in society without being self-conscious.*

I was never a big party girl. Although I drank a bit, especially in college, I've never done drugs, smoked pot, or even tried cigarettes.

I'm not telling you to get into drugs; just lighten up and push your envelope a little. After your vision quest, maybe go to Burning Man, that big, artsy, free-for-all in the desert. Dress up in funky costumes or run around naked. When you get home, go out dancing. Just go have fun.

Another tree chimes in: *Yeah, girl, you need to lift your lid!*

A bush agrees: *Let more of yourself out and more of others in.*

A heart-shaped stump adds: *Stop worrying so much about being liked.*

This is like the out-of-control mop scene from *Fantasia*. If my East coast friends and family could see me now, they would think I've lost my mind. I can't believe I'm listening to foliage. But they have a point—it all seems to come down to my fear of rejection.

It's not an unfounded fear; I've had a history of being rejected for being completely myself. In school, when I eagerly participated and excelled at academics, sports, music, and drama, the cool kids tormented me, calling me "Little Miss Perfect." It was like being in that game, Whac-a-Mole. Each time I stuck out by doing well, I became the mole—the others would pound me as hard and fast as they could. Years later, while Philippe was initially fascinated with my out-of-the-box spiritual approach, he ultimately broke up with me for not sharing his more traditional religious beliefs. Being fully myself could mean being mocked or being alone.

On the other hand, others also appreciate and respect my unique way of being. I met tons of other out-of-the-ordinary friends at Harvard, who felt more like "my people." The trees are right. If repressing my less socially acceptable self is preventing me from fully experiencing life, it's time to cut myself loose. I smile as I envision future encounters between my uninhibited self and my most conservative colleagues and family. "Laurie the Freak." I can't wait to try that one on for size.

"What else do I need to know?" I ask the Death and Rebirth Tree.

Let's talk about your true nature. How would you describe yourself?

"Well, when I was little, people would always say that I was a 'good kid.' I liked helping others and doing the right thing. How am I as an adult? I like to laugh and see the lighter side of life, I guess, and I still like helping others . . . "

Yes, you are a humorous healer, it interrupts. *This is your true nature, and it is a very good way to be. What you need to be aware of is when you're using it as a schtick.*

"A *schtick?*" I ask, amused. Apparently, this tree speaks Yiddish.

Yes, a schtick means "an act," using your talents or traits to either entertain or to secure recognition or attention.

"I know what a schtick is," I laugh, "I'm just not clear on exactly what you mean."

When people are being themselves, their true qualities show and flow naturally in each situation. However, people have become too aware of how others perceive them. Be careful not to use your "good kid" or "humorous healer" nature or any other qualities as a persona when you are not genuinely in that place, simply because you feel it is expected or because you think it will bring you recognition. If you do, you will feel unfulfilled and disconnected, both from yourself and from whomever you're trying to fool or impress.

I nod. I'm keenly aware of when I'm acting to create a certain impression versus being my real self. If there's one skill I'd like to unlearn, it's the art of wearing masks.

As I stand up to go, the stump says, *One more thing. It's wonderful that you have a lot of energy. But if you don't direct it well, it's all for nothing.*

And try not to be such a perfectionist, the bush adds.

Okay, that's enough, everyone, says the Death and Rebirth Tree. *You can come back tomorrow, Laurie, and we can talk more then.*

I press my hands together and bow to my new plant friends.

Nature is a powerful teacher, if one is wise enough to listen.

Circling the Truth
Command Fear, Release Anger, and Call Self-Pity's Bluff

"Ouch! What the . . . ?" I awake to the alarm clock of a red ant stinging my right hand. Aside from the sting, though, I feel good. The first day of fasting was rough, but after about forty hours with no food, my body feels incredibly light, and my mind is crystal clear. I'm moving a little more slowly than usual, but I have a surprising amount of energy given the complete lack of calories. When I get an occasional hunger pang or feel a little dizzy, drinking water makes it go away.

"Another day in paradise," I yawn, blinking into the daylight like a gopher crawling out of its hole. "And—whoo—another day hotter than hell." The average summer daytime temperature in the Chama desert is 108 degrees, 95 in the shade. Good thing I brought tons of SPF 50, though I should've brought the waterproof kind, the way I'm dripping. On the other hand, it feels kind of purifying to sweat like this.

I rummage through my pack, looking for my notes from Sparrow's orientation. Nope, nothing; I must've left them back at basecamp. In a way, that's better. Without them, I'll be forced to act spontaneously and from the heart while I perform the rituals, rather than ticking items off of a "spiritual to-do list."

The first ritual that pops into my head is the "Truth Mandala." The purpose of this ritual is to access and release our deepest emotions, especially the difficult ones. I pick up a stick and draw a big circle on the ground, dividing it into quarters. In the first quadrant, I write the word "ANGER," in the second, "FEAR," in the third, "GRIEF," and in the fourth, "JEALOUSY." In the center of the circle, intersecting all of the quadrants, I draw a smaller circle in which I write, "HOPE."

I step into the fear quadrant. Looking out over the canyon, I feel myself stalling, because I already know where I need to go. Hands down, the mother of all my fears is the fear of not being lovable. I close my eyes to let myself feel that fear. Next thing I know, I'm fifteen years old again.

Slumped against my high school locker, I convulsed with the kind of sobs that only come from the deepest part of the soul.

My best friend Jared had just ditched me. He dropped the bomb over the phone.

"If you can't go with the crowd, you're gonna be on your own."

"So, if I don't join in drinking and backstabbing with the others, we're done as friends?" I couldn't believe it.

"You never had any friends," he said. (Click . . . dial tone).

You never had any friends. His words stabbed straight through my heart.

For the next several months, it was a struggle just to get through each day. I isolated myself from my peers and my family. I was angry and depressed, alternating between waves of shame and self-righteousness. My former friends watched and did nothing. The people who disliked me reveled in my decline. Most of my other classmates didn't even notice. My family didn't "do" emotions, so I couldn't confide in them. Thoughts of suicide began crossing my mind.

Thank goodness for my diary. Every day, I wrote to cheerlead myself out of my well of despair: *"Two inches up, one back—that's okay, I'm making progress. I can do this; I won't be feeling this way forever. Fight, Laurie, c'mon, FIGHT! Just a couple more years of high school, then it's on to greener pastures . . ."*

If it weren't for my diary, there's a good chance I wouldn't be here today.

⌢

I open my eyes and look down at the mandala. My heart is racing a mile a minute. Gripped by the primal "fight or flight" response, I feel my whole body tense up and get ready to flee.

"Breathe, Laurie. This will pass," I try reassuring myself.

But it's too late. I'm besieged by my worst fears: *You're not worthy. Nobody likes you. You're fat and ugly. You suck as a leader.*

"*Breathe.* Stay in the present." I try again to calm myself.

You'll never find true love; there's nobody out there for you! You're going to die poor, sick, and all by yourself, because nobody loves you! I clutch my heart and gasp for breath. *Oh God, I don't want to die alone.*

I inhale deeply and pry off each of my fears. "Stay there!" I command them, stepping out of the quadrant and pointing to the ground.

Heart still pounding, I enter the anger quadrant. I can't remember the last time I let myself get really pissed off.

I stand quietly and wait. After a few minutes, I see the faces of all the friends who betrayed me, lovers who lied to me, colleagues who put me down. They pass through my memory one by one in a painful parade. I'm not sure what to do. I start by calmly describing to each of them why I feel wronged. But by the third person, my voice is heated. Soon, I'm screaming.

"You spineless coward!" I shout at the image of Jared standing outside of our high school. "What kind of a loser dumps his best friend to fit in with the crowd?"

"You call yourself my friend?" I yell at a graduate school buddy who tried to seduce Philippe.

"How dare you blame me for everything," I glare at an employee. "Did it ever occur to you that *you* might be doing something to cause this situation?"

An ex-boyfriend comes into view. "You told me you'd never loved anyone the way you love me. You said I was *special.*" I choke on angry tears. "Two weeks after we break up, and you're already dating someone else? Just how *special* do you think that makes me feel?"

What's coming out of me is ugly, but I need to set it loose. At the time these things occurred, I said nothing to those who hurt me.

I step into the grief quadrant, fall to my knees, and sob. Underneath the anger is an even deeper sadness. As the hurt and grief come bubbling out of me, I realize it all leads back to my core wound of feeling unlovable. I weep for a good long while, creating a spreading patch of wet dirt beneath me.

Then, suddenly, I start cracking up. "For God's sake you're pathetic! *Poor you, you've been so wronged . . . poor you, nobody loves you.* What a load of crap!"

"Yes, some people don't like you, and some even hate you. Get over it! Others like you a lot and even love you. You're never going to be liked by everyone, nor will you like everyone else. You're not a bad person on either count. Just do your best not to take it personally and have compassion both for others and yourself."

I feel a heavy rock lift off of my heart as it all becomes clear. Feeling unlovable is my illusion. Feeling sorry for myself is keeping me stuck in grief.

I exhale, full of gratitude and relief. All this time, I've been causing my own suffering. I brush myself off and walk over to the word "hope."

Cross-Examining the Judge
Get to the Root of Judgment

Having just moved past my grief, I'm now eager to move past my fear. But how?

My inner voice chimes in to help. *Most of your fears are related to judgment. You fear you're not lovable and worthy, because you grew up in an environment where people were judgmental and critical, both of you and others. You've carried that judgment into adulthood. When you're not criticizing yourself, you're worried that others are judging you, and you attract those people into your life to confirm your theory. You're sometimes so specific that you attract people who judge you in the exact same way that you judge yourself.*

As the truth wells up, so again do my tears. Judgment is a huge issue for me. Not only am I hyper-sensitive to being judged, but I also judge others. Sometimes, I get caught in a judgment "double-whammy:" I judge others, then judge myself for judging them. Often, it turns into a triple-header, as I then judge myself for judging myself.

"But don't people always judge? It seems like human nature."

Yes, but the key is to use judgment in a helpful, rather than hurtful, way. When you view judgment in the sense of discernment, it is in fact an essential skill. In order to survive, we need to discern whether we're physically safe. Also in emotional contexts, we need to assess whether or not to trust certain people and situations. But when we use our discernment to unduly criticize others or ourselves, it becomes destructive. It's this type of judgment you want to keep in check.

"This is all very true and helpful, but how can it help me to move past my fear?"

Judgment is often a reactive defense mechanism against a deeper fear. The next time you find yourself judging yourself or others, ask yourself, "What's my underlying fear that's been triggered?"

I thought about the time that a work colleague gave me a harsh evaluation on my annual review. At the time, I reacted by judging him back, declaring his feedback to be unbalanced and unfair. Looking back now, I can see that he triggered my fear of not being good enough.

And You, Brutus?
Forgive Betrayal and Other Injustices

Only one piece to go, moving past my anger. This part feels hard. I don't want to play the victim and blame others, but things have been done to me that aren't okay. I don't want to let people walk all over me, but I also don't want to spend my life stuck in anger over the past.

Of all the ways I've been hurt, betrayal has been the toughest to get over and has taken the longest to heal. It always feels so unexpected and shocking when someone I deeply love and trust harms me for his or her own advantage.

"So how can we forgive people who have wronged us? How can we truly let it go? Is that even possible?"

"They know not what they do," comes an answer from the Golden Cliffs this time. *Whether people betray you, abandon you, blame you, or put you down, they're doing the best they can from where they are in their personal growth and level of awareness at that moment.*

I think of the ex-boyfriend who jumped into bed with another woman soon after we broke up. Years later, he apologized to me. After four failed marriages, he had learned many important lessons about his addiction to women. People do grow and change in their own time.

"Any other strategies to help me forgive?"

A cloud passes over the sun, causing the cliffs to get dark, then bright again, almost like a blink. *Sacred contracts,* I hear the same voice say.

We make agreements with people before we're born to help us learn our lessons in this lifetime. These contracts can be with those who've agreed to love and support us, as well as those whose contract it is to hurt us deeply.

That was an eye-opener. I'd made a contract with several people to betray and hurt me in various ways so I could learn how to forgive. I should be grateful, not angry; they upheld their part of the agreement beautifully.

From "You Suck" to "I Rock"
Move Past Jealousy

I start erasing the mandala with my foot when I realize I skipped the jealousy quadrant. Interesting.

I step into the quadrant, breathing in and out quietly, and ponder when and why I get jealous. I don't have the "keeping up with the Jones" syndrome; I don't covet other people's status or stuff. My brand of jealousy is of people who get more attention or compliments. I sit there resenting them, wishing it were me.

One time at an Esalen workshop, I felt bitter toward the teacher's pet. The teacher kept calling on this young woman and complimenting her contributions, as if each thing she said were brilliant. *She's hogging the floor,* I thought, *he should really give someone else a chance to speak.* In another workshop, a woman wore low-cut dresses to each session, and all of the men fawned over her. *She's not that cute,* I kept thinking to myself.

"Why do I have to be like that?" I ask whichever of my nature friends is willing to answer.

It comes down to self-esteem, comes the answer from the rocky bluffs. *To move beyond jealousy, accept in your heart that you're a beautiful, talented person, whether or not you receive external validation. When you recognize your own worth, you won't care whether anyone pays attention to you or not. You won't need a teacher to confirm you're special, nor a man's compliments to know you're pretty.*

A wave of confidence and exhilaration bubbles up in me.

"I'm a red hot mama in the Canyon of the Strong Women!" I whoop.

I pick up my rattle and start rattling it hard, hopping around and laughing. Soon, I'm making up joyful songs, half singing and half shouting. Native Americans call these "medicine" or "soul" songs. I dance wildly as I shake my rattle and bang on my water bottle like it's a drum.

I can only imagine what I'd look and sound like to some poor forest ranger wandering by. But who cares? I'm having a blast. I'm a "freak" having a private party, experiencing uninhibited fun for the first time in years.

I step out of the Truth Mandala, exhausted and elated. I feel like I just received an emotional heart transplant, replacing the old heart with a new one that feels much lighter and freer in my body.

8

DOWNLOAD IN THE DESERT

I *need to write this stuff down.* I grab my journal, hoping to capture as many of the Truth Mandala lessons as I can while they're still fresh on my mind.

But wait, where's my favorite pen? I'm fussy about my pens, especially when I'm writing in a diary—the ink has to flow as freely as my thoughts.

The last time I focused so much on my pen was at a Kabbalah-inspired homeopathy workshop I attended three years ago. For twelve days, we turned bits of plants into medicines with a mortar and pestle, while our leader guided us through the four Jewish mystical realms. On the last day, we did a special midnight mixing. At 3:00 a.m., I looked down into my bowl and saw the pen I use to write in my journal. Did I drop it in there? Impossible, my journal and pen were back in my room. As I continued staring into the bowl, more and more pens started appearing, until the bottom of the bowl was covered with them. Then, like a scene from Harry Potter, my paternal grandfather, who died before I was born, looked up at me from the bottom of the bowl, opened his mouth, and said, "Write."

A few months ago, I received a package from my Aunt Joan. I hadn't been in touch with her for years. Inside the parcel was a blank leather journal with a Post-it note that said simply, "Write— anything!"

I lean against the Sentinel Tree, and suddenly, it all makes sense: the pens in the bowl, Aunt Joan's Post-it, and my gnawing feeling of needing to do something more. I understand now what I'm supposed to do out here.

Overcome with the urge to write, I open my journal. A single word comes out, as the title of a book:

SHINE

I ponder what that word means. For me, to "shine" means to be your brightest, most authentic self, living a life that's fun, full, and free. I look back at my own life; there were times when I shone and times when I hid my light. What was happening for me when I took the brave, exhilarating steps to follow my dreams, and what was going on when I held myself back? How can the lessons I learned help guide others?

Immediately, a new title appears:

~~*SHINE*~~
THE ROAD TO SHINE

Ah, I get it. This book is about *how* to shine, how to get to your fullest, best life. Three distinct steps appear in my mind's eye . . . a roadmap.

Soon, words come pouring out of me. I can barely move the pen fast enough to keep up. This must be what people call "automatic writing" or "channeling." All I know is that it feels like the book is writing itself.

Chapter One
Step One—Uncover and Heal Your Lack of Self-Love

To be the person you want to be and have that life you really want, you first need to figure out how and why you're holding yourself back. You've got to get to the root. Many of us blame our fears, our unhealthy thoughts and behaviors, and the traits we're not proud of as the culprits that are keeping us down. But underlying all of those is something even deeper: lack of self-love.

Some reading this will cringe at that "touchy feely" phrase and decide it doesn't apply to them. For others it may resonate, but they may not yet be sure how it is playing out in their lives.

Here are the most common signs of lack of self-love:
*Addictive behaviors: Anything we use or do to escape inner pain temporarily. In addition to alcohol and other drugs, we can be addicted to work, sex, exercise, or TV—whatever we use to distract ourselves from doing the deeper work that could permanently make us feel better.

* **Putting others before ourselves:** Altruism in balance is a good thing, but for those of us who put ourselves second and rarely get our needs or desires met, it's time to stop and take the "doormat" test. Do you think your needs and desires aren't as important as those of others? Do you feel you don't deserve to have your needs met? Are you feeling resentful, but still refuse to speak up? If the answer is yes, it's time to get up off the floor.

* **Looking for external validation:** For example, we don't feel lovable unless we're in a romantic relationship or getting compliments from others. Or we depend on constant recognition from friends or family, bosses, and colleagues for our successes to feel good about ourselves.

* **Focusing on others' opinions:** Spending far too much time worrying what people think of us. Fearful of being judged as deficient in some way, we live according to what others and society say we "should" do rather than allowing ourselves to make decisions based on what feels right and good to us.

* **Not speaking our truth:** Not expressing our true emotions for fear of being rejected. We go

along agreeably with what others want us to do or let people put words in our mouths.

*Reopening old wounds: Some people avoid their emotional wounds while others mire themselves in them and get stuck. We've all been wronged and hurt by others, and our pain is legitimate. However, if we constantly retell ourselves and others our negative stories, it's like we repeatedly rip the scab off of a wound so it cannot heal. Even if it eventually heals, it'll leave a nasty scar.

*Inability to forgive: When we've been betrayed, neglected, or subjected to physical or emotional harm, it can be hard to forgive. Often, we want revenge. But the irony is that we are the ones who suffer most when we don't forgive. More likely than not, the people who've hurt us have moved on with their lives—some may not even realize what they did.

*Self-righteous anger: When we find ourselves having murderous thoughts about the grandma in the next lane who cut us off, it's time to take a look at what's really going on. Anger often masks hurt or fear. It's easier to blame someone or something than to examine which of our underlying buttons were pushed and to learn how not to be so reactive.

*Chronic pain: Sometimes there are strictly physical causes for pain, but often, emotional wounds are the real cause of chronic discomfort. I've had countless experiences with clients whose chronic physical pain improved radically once we got to the emotional or spiritual problem that was manifesting in the body.

*Not letting people in: Some of us can't show our vulnerable sides even to our partners, family members, and friends. We feel as though we have a "wall" or "shell" around us. Some guarding is healthy until we know whom we can trust. However, if we struggle with making eye contact or with intimate conversations, it's a telltale sign we may need to let a few trusted people "storm the castle." Ironically, once we do, we often feel stronger and more protected than before.

*Boredom or restlessness: This symptom of lack of self-love stems from not asking ourselves what really makes us tick and how we'd like to actively "be" in the world. Instead, we feel that our lives don't really matter, and so we go from job to job, relationship to relationship, experience to experience, feeling empty and wondering why we're here.

*Selling ourselves short: There are many ways we sabotage ourselves: staying in a job we hate for fear of not getting another one, settling for romantic relationships and friendships where we don't feel fully understood or supported, preventing ourselves from experiencing success by not trying in the first place. We sell ourselves short due to self-doubt, fear of failure, or success, fear of change, and perhaps by approaching life fearfully in general. Meanwhile, we'll soon discover that people value us in direct proportion to how much we value ourselves.

*Putting yourself down: Listen to yourself as you speak such telltale phrases as, "This probably sounds stupid . . . ," "You're probably going to think I'm weird, but . . . ," etc. Self-deprecating comments are one of the many ways we judge ourselves harshly and a clear sign that we're not valuing ourselves very highly. We may think we're only joking, but all humor has some truth to it.

*Bragging or overachieving: It manifests as the opposite of putting ourselves down, selling ourselves short, and underachieving, but boasting or overachieving can also be ways of compensating for the same fundamental lack of love and worthiness we feel inside.

*Taking things personally: When people say and do unkind things to us, it's ultimately about their own triggers and underlying issues. But often we don't recognize this, especially when the criticism is aimed right at us. Even when it isn't directed at us, we may "read in" negative personal feedback or judgment that wasn't intended by the speaker at all. In these cases, we are the ones judging ourselves.

*Feeling depressed and lonely: Depression can cause us to feel so badly about ourselves that we don't even have the energy to get out of bed and face the day. As a result, we withdraw from others and feel alone. If we're not careful, we'll forget altogether that we are good, lovable souls who are loved by more people around us than we realize.

*Playing the martyr: Many of us try to feel better about ourselves by showing the world how much we sacrifice and suffer. We've likely all known someone who complains about how awful his or her job or relationship is, yet never follows anyone's advice on how to make it better.

When we're truly unhappy but don't make changes to improve our situation, it's time to ask what sort of pay-off we might be getting from feeling like we're suffering more than anyone else.

*Difficulty setting and sticking to boundaries: We may feel guilty about saying no, even when we know we should. We may do this to avoid confrontation or because it's easier to just do what the other person wants. When we have trouble drawing a line, or we easily move it or step over it, we're ultimately telling ourselves that we don't deserve to have what we want. Ensuring that our needs are met is not selfish; in fact, it's critical to being able to love, support, and help others.

*Frequent anxiety: Anxiety reflects a lack of trust in ourselves, others, and the world. It's also about needing to feel in control. The more we build our self-esteem, learn to hear and follow our intuition, and let go of our need to drive the outcome of every situation, the more confident we become and the less scary of a place the world turns out to be. A helpful mantra is, "Everything is happening the way it should, ultimately in my best interest."

Any of these ringing a bell, for yourself or anyone you know? I'm telling you, lack of self-love is a silent epidemic. Now let's go even deeper.

This next statement may surprise you. (It was certainly an eye-opener for me.) We cause our own fear, anger, and grief.

When you are suffering and want to stop feeling unhappy, the first thing to do is look at how you're causing your own distress. A good indicator that the problem may lie with you is when you notice that you keep getting wronged in the same way or that other people don't get upset about the same things in the way you do.

There are three common ways in which people avoid dealing with the underlying causes of their unhappiness: self-pity, judgment, and self-sabotage.

It's often easier to feel sorry for ourselves than to take care of our problems. Unwitting friends may try to help us problem-solve, not realizing that we are not really ready or willing to move forward. We're either getting too much out of our pity party, or we lack the confidence to confront someone or to make a change.

Judgment is another avoidance tactic. "I'm not the loser; he or she is!" We describe all the ways in which another person is messed up, so we don't have to look at our own shortcomings and how badly we feel about them. We may also turn this judgment on ourselves as a pre-emptive strike. Subconsciously, we put ourselves down before anyone else can.

Finally, we may keep ourselves feeling bad through self-sabotage. Although it's a disempowering way of being in the world, we may decide it's easier to stay in the comfortable place of being a failure than to try to succeed. "I don't have to risk losing if I never get in the game," we figure. Others muster the courage to take positive steps in the right direction, then freak out and derail things when it looks like they may actually succeed. "This might be that healthy, true love relationship I've always dreamed of. Quick, mess it up!"

So how do we stop doing all this so we can be happier?

To move on from self-sabotage, ask yourself one key question each time you need to make a decision: "Will doing this move me closer to or further from where I want to be?"

To free yourself from fear of judgment, adopt the attitude of that book title, _What You Think of Me Is None of My Business._

To free yourself from self-pity and the accompanying anger and grief, you've got to stop playing the victim. People who view life through the "poor me" lens constantly focus on the ways they're being wronged, picking out data and forging interpretations to support themselves in the role of the victim. They exclude or downplay information that would cause them to have to question or change that comfortable, albeit emotionally unhealthy, worldview. The good news is that we can "rewire" ourselves by choosing to see things through a different lens. Once we stop feeling sorry for ourselves, we realize that feeling unlovable and unworthy is all our own biased, distorted interpretation—like looking at the world through a funhouse mirror. If you want to lift the weight of sadness off your heart, stop paying admission to the dark carnival.

Ultimately, the power to grow and change lies within us, and no one can give or take away that power.

I put down my pen and ponder what to write next.

So far, I've spent a lot of time talking about the place where you *don't* want to be and how to get out, and not much time on the place where you *do* want to be and how to get there. It's not enough to know what we want to escape from; we must also know where we want to go to. So the question now is "*How* can we feel more lovable and worthy?"

The Top Ten Steps to Self-Love

1. Do nice things for yourself (and don't be cheap about it).

2. Don't let anyone else's negativity harm your spirit.

3. Express your true feelings and needs, even when judged or met with resistance.

4. Only share your gifts with those who appreciate them.

5. Don't limit yourself or settle in any area of your life, even when you're afraid.

6. Stay balanced in giving and taking; don't over-give, and allow yourself to receive.

7. Listen closely to your "dark side"; it has a lot to teach you.

8. Lighten up; don't take yourself and life so seriously.

9. Honor yourself by setting boundaries and sticking to them.

10. Trust your gut; your intuition will always guide you well.

After taking some or all of these steps to increase self-love, the last logical question becomes, "How do we know when we get there?"

I conclude Chapter One:

You'll know you've achieved healthy self-love when there's no more emotional charge with the people who've hurt you—you've let it go and moved on. Another sign is when you regain the levity, joy, and spontaneity of your childhood—you can be yourself without caring or even noticing what anyone else thinks. Finally, a critical clue that you've completed this stage is the heartfelt realization that you are fully lovable, even when others can't fully love you.

I got so caught up in writing that I almost miss my turn at the stone pile—the safety system on our vision quest. Buddying up with whomever ends up closest to our solo fasting location (in my case, Annie), we choose a spot halfway between our two sites where we make and then adjust a rock pile twice a day. The stone pile design can be fancy or simple, so long as it's obvious the stones have been moved. Should you arrive to the stone pile and see that your buddy hasn't moved the rocks, you know to go check on him or her. One person takes the morning shift, and the other goes in the afternoon. Not being a morning person, I volunteered for the late shift. Annie and I chose a spot along a dry river creek right beneath a towering, charred tree we nicknamed the "Lightning Tree."

By the time I get back, it's already time for bed. Besides that brief stone pile break, I'd spent all day writing.

⌒

I love my bathroom view. This morning as I gaze down at the valley, I see something odd. Standing out from all the other trees, there's one that's glowing in the sun. As if someone were shining a spotlight on it, it seems to be inviting me to take a closer look.

I head down the mountain to the canyon floor. I soon discover that it's much farther away than it looked from my campsite. As I get closer, I come upon a steep ravine that cuts off the path to the tree. My heart sinks. Then, to my amazement, I notice a well-worn cow trail stretching from directly in front of me down the ravine and back up the other side, forging a safe passage.

Approaching the tree, I see that it's in fact a circle of six trees. There's one opening in the ring. Sensing that this place is for me, I step into it.

Welcome to the Circle of Elders, the trees say. *It is time for you to take your place as a spiritual teacher, to guide others to their light and purpose, as you have been guided to yours.*

"Come again?" I ask. "A spiritual teacher? What, like Gandhi or Buddha?"

Instantly, I'm flooded with self-doubt. I guess they mean more of a modern-day spiritual teacher, like the insightful people whose CDs I listened to and whose workshops I attended. But still, I'm supposed to join this circle of today's esteemed, inspirational teachers? I feel lucky when they autograph my book. Am I truly ready to share all that I've learned in the role of a teacher?

I flash back to an appointment at a career services office twenty years ago.

"Harvard grad, eh?" the man behind the desk asked me, flipping through my file.

"Yes, sir."

"Come from a medical family."

"Uh huh."

"Just back from a big world trip, I see?"

I nodded. I was trying to figure out "what I want to be when I grow up."

"Well, let's see what the results tell us," he said, pulling out my score sheets from the personality and career aptitude tests I had just taken.

"All the results point toward 'teacher, healer, guide,'" he declared.

I laughed. "You mean, I'm going to be some sort of TV evangelist or woo woo hippie guru?"

"Whatever you make of it," he replied, "$75 please."

I walked out of the career office, shaking my head in disbelief. *Dude, I'm a spiritual teacher. Try floating that around a cocktail party.* "What do you do, Laurie?" "I'm in the wisdom business . . . yourself?" *Yeah, right.*

Little did I know that I would in fact spend the next fifteen years as a teacher, healer, and guide, in the forms of a wilderness instructor, high school teacher and administrator, public education reformer, massage therapist, energy healer, and now perhaps, as some sort of a spiritual coach.

Take one of our leaves, as a reminder of your place in the Circle, one of the Elder trees offers.

And use that broken branch lying underneath me as a walking stick if you become weaker during your fast, another one suggests.

I hug each trunk in the circle and thank them for their message.

As I head to the stone pile, I ponder the Elders' powerful directive. It strikes me as an enormous task. It's been hard enough working on my own personal growth for all these years. This would be a big leap to make—leaving my public education career and becoming a spiritual teacher.

On the other hand, it also seems like a natural extension of what I've already been doing for two decades. This would just be a new branch on my path as an educator, teaching others how to reach their full potential.

By the time I return to the campsite, I shift from, "That's scary—why me?" to "Well, why *not* me?" I enjoy writing and speaking, and I'm passionate about personal growth. I'm as good of a candidate as the next guy, right?

Even though I have mixed emotions, on the deepest level of my soul I know what just happened. I have confirmed my life purpose.

I grab my journal and start writing again.

Chapter Two
Step Two—Discover Your Passion and Purpose

Once you've addressed your lack of self-love, it's time to discover your life purpose. This does not necessarily refer to your particular job or career or anything specific you might do to manifest your purpose. By purpose, I mean what your gifts are to the world, "what you came here to do" in the broadest sense.

How do you go about finding your purpose? Start by asking yourself a few key questions:

*What am I most passionate about?

*What would I most like to do if I didn't have to worry about money or relationships?

*If I were to die tomorrow, what legacy would I
 like to leave?

It's never too late to begin this quest. Grandma
Moses began painting when she was almost eighty
years old.

Some people have always known their purpose and
have spent their whole lives fulfilling it. Others knew
their passion at childhood but had it squashed out
of them by their parents or by their own self-doubt.
I have one friend who knew since he was a little
boy that he was an artist. But his dad felt that
art wasn't "manly" enough and pushed him to play
sports instead. By the time he was of working age,
he doubted his own artistic abilities and became a
painting contractor instead, which he also felt would
be more financially sustainable. Only now, at age
thirty-nine, is he coming into his artist self, joyfully
acknowledging his love of photography, deciding
to go back to school to become a professional
photographer.

Meanwhile, most of us are born without being aware
of our passions and purpose, and it is something
we have to discover or remember at some point
along the way. Some people fear that they have no

purpose or passions at all. For them, the process becomes about taking away the shroud to find out who they really are.

The good news is that God or the Universe—or whatever you call your Higher Power—gives us signs along the way. Our job is to pay attention and follow both earthly and divine signs designed to guide us along our spiritual path.

In order to be able to notice these signs, you'll need to develop certain traits and skills.

First, you must be able to receive, as well as take. So many people have difficulty receiving. We give and give to others tirelessly. Yet even when we are exhausted, we say, "No thanks" to those who offer help. I can do this myself, you might think; I don't really need help. But just because you can do something doesn't mean you have to. Allowing yourself to receive isn't about what you are or are not capable of; it's about letting someone give to you and accepting the gift. Not only do you deserve to receive; you need to receive. In order to be an empowered, self-loving person who is going to step into and fulfill his or her highest life purpose, you must be able to balance giving and receiving.

You must also be able to take. While receiving is allowing yourself to accept a gift and let it come into your space, taking is actively seeking out something you need or want—taking the initiative to bring it into your space. This may mean taking more time off work or spending more money on yourself than you normally do, or perhaps carving out time for yourself in your day or week that you would usually spend on others.

Both receiving and taking with joy and gratitude, not guilt and resistance, are fundamental shifts that must occur before you are ready to discover your life purpose. If you cannot openly receive into your heart and mind, you will either reject important signs that are pointing you toward your path or you will miss them altogether.

After opening yourself to receive the signs, you must trust yourself to recognize and follow them. How many times have you thought to yourself, What an amazing coincidence! Or perhaps you unexpectedly received a piece of information at the exact time you most needed it. Rather than dismissing these as mere chance, consider them serendipitous signs that you're on the right path. It's important to follow the signs even when you're not yet clear about what they mean. When you have enough trust to follow them, inevitably, their meaning will become clear.

To make the most of your signs, you must be able to interpret them from a place of your own inner knowing. All too often, we look to outside sources to find the meaning of things. Debbie Ford had a wonderful way of helping people access their ability to make their own meaning: At her workshops, whenever someone said, "I don't know (what this dream means, what to do, etc.)," she immediately responded, "And if you *did* know?" Ten times out of ten, the person was then able to answer his or her own question.

Once you recognize and follow the signs that point you in the direction of your life purpose, you can then choose how to manifest your purpose in the world. There are many ways you can be your true self. For example, my own purpose is to help people live more fully. To do this, I may write books, teach workshops, or do one-on-one counseling. Maybe I'll do it for a living or maybe in my spare time. The specifics will evolve and unfold as I manifest my life purpose in different ways at different times.

With my photographer friend, he's only recently

begun manifesting his true artist self in the form of a photography career. But long before this point, he was going through the world as an artist, taking photos and doing other art projects for fun. In his previous career, his housepainting work displayed some of the most beautiful colors and creative paint jobs I had ever seen. His passion is to create and see beauty in everything around him; this is his life purpose.

Compared to healing your lack of self-love, getting clarity on your purpose may be easier and take less time, because it's primarily about remembering what you already know. You'll realize you've discovered or remembered your purpose when you feel clear about the way you can and want to contribute to the world. You calmly say to yourself, against all fears and doubts, Why not this? Who better to do this than me?

Unbelievable. It's bedtime again. Our solo fasting time is whizzing by. I can't believe it's already the end of day three. I blow a kiss good night to the blackness all around me as I quickly succumb to sleep.

⁀

Oh, gross, my sleeping bag is all wet! I awake with a jolt and flip on my headlamp. It's pouring rain, and it's still completely dark. I can see my white, curling breath; it's a really cold night. Four streams of water are running downhill onto where I'm sleeping. Water is also dripping on my head. I shine my light up at the tarp; there are dozens of pinholes in the plastic I hadn't noticed before.

I manage to stop the leaking by building a new layer of tarp underneath the original one using garbage bags and duct tape. With my hiking boots, some rocks, and my water jugs, I create a mini-retaining wall to halt the flow of water. "Move over, MacGyver!" I smile when I'm done.

As long as I'm wide awake, I decide to do another ritual. "Calling in the Dark" is a night ritual where you confront each of your "demons" and negotiate with them. The purpose is to face your deepest fears, rather than to keep pushing them away.

I close my eyes and say out loud, "Okay, demons, show yourselves!" A frightening image appears—a horrible, hairy black tarantula with an eagle's head.

Scared and repulsed, I ask, "Who are you?"

I'm your fear of your own power.

"What do you want from me?"

I want you to give up your power.

Sparrow said not to be frightened during this ritual, to simply refuse to give the demon what it wants. We should ask it what else it might want, until we find something we feel comfortable giving it.

"I'm sorry, I can't do that. What else do you want?"

Then I need you to step fully into your power.

Sparrow also taught us to ask the demon for a gift in return for doing its bidding.

"What will you give me in return?"

The courage to do so.

Then the demon disappears.

"Well, this is it," I gulp. The last night of a vision quest is the most powerful one, especially if you choose to engage in a culminating ritual called the "Purpose Circle." For this ritual, you draw a circle on the ground about six feet across representing your life purpose. There, you will stay from sunset until the following sunrise, crying out all night long for a vision of your purpose. When you step out of the circle, you are "rebirthed" with a new understanding of who you are and what you will be contributing to the world.

There is no doubt in my mind where I should draw my Purpose Circle. As I prepare to leave my camping spot and hike up to the Golden Cliffs, I wonder what will happen tonight. I've already experienced so much over the past few days. I've shifted and healed many deep fears and wounds. I've discovered my life purpose as a spiritual teacher. I'm writing a book. What more could there possibly be to come?

The long trek to the Golden Cliffs seems even longer after four days without food. I have to stop and rest several times, but safely and surely, I arrive at my spot. The Circle of Elders made a good call with the walking stick. I lean on it all the way up the mountain.

Scouting for the best location to draw the circle, I decide to place it next to the Death and Rebirth Tree, appreciating its symbolism even more. I set up a simple circle with each of the four directions of the Medicine Wheel (north, south, east, and west) marked by rocks and trees. My six-foot circle exactly fits the width of the narrow ridge.

The sun is setting. I feel a sense of completion as well as anticipation at what's to come. I take off my boots and socks so I can feel the red, powdery earth with my bare feet. I grab my rattle, take a deep breath, and enter the circle.

Crash! No sooner do I step into the circle than the most powerful storm I have ever experienced hits with full force. The sky goes from sunset colors to pitch black in a matter of seconds. I'm besieged by gale force winds, pelting rain, bullets of hail, and lightning bolts crashing all around. Within minutes, my clothes are soaked through, and I'm up to my ankles in red mud. It's freezing cold. I dig my toes deep into the mud to keep from getting blown off the ridge.

I sway, stomp, and sing to keep myself from passing out. I do jumping jacks, hop up and down, and step from side to side again and again. A few times, I step out of the circle to climb up and down the left hill of the saddle until I can feel my feet and fingers again.

After a few hours, I start a conversation with the Higher Powers. God, Moses, Jesus, Mohammed, Buddha, Zeus . . . I'm calling out to all of them. I figure any deity who'll listen will do.

I begin negotiating with them: "Why can't you give me your messages under the tarp at my campsite—or back home in my nice, warm garden in Berkeley? Why have you brought me all the way up here in the middle of a freezing storm?"

You're being tested. This time, the voice feels like it's coming from both outside and inside me.

"Tested for what?" I ask.

The voice explains that I'm being tested to see if I'm truly committed to stepping into my purpose. It says that the work I've chosen to do—helping people to spiritually transform—will be a much greater challenge than surviving the rain, hail, and cold for one night. It cautions that people don't like to change, especially when it comes to their most deeply held beliefs about themselves and the world.

"Do you think I can't do it, then?"

No one doubts you, but sometimes you're too soft. You need to toughen up.

I understand. Somehow, that's all I need. So long as there's a reason that I'm in this storm, I know I can get through it.

At one point in the late-night sky, I see a cloud shaped like a lion reclining with his lioness.

"What does that mean?" I ask the Higher Powers.

To fulfill your purpose, you must regain confidence in yourself as a leader. Know that some people will condemn you and seek to do you harm. But you must not give up.

Great, I've apparently signed up for a lifetime of Whac-a-Mole.

"Do I have to keep putting myself out there?"

Your station in life is to lead. Others are counting on you.

I sure hope this hailstorm will toughen me up, then. Right now, I don't have the stomach for this leadership stuff. Maybe I'll have an easier time of it in the love life department.

"Will I ever find true love?" I ask.

You have more healing to do first, the voice responds. *For now, don't get swept up in your emotions, especially yearning. Your emotions will come and go, like waves of the ocean. When a wave crashes at your feet, your inner wisdom will help you stand firm until it subsides back to sea.*

I have one more important question. "How do I forgive those who have hurt me? I don't want to go home still feeling resentment."

Look for the lessons they have taught you, the gifts they each have brought you.

One by one, I call aloud the names of the people who've hurt me and look for the gift. One taught me to stay true to myself, even through painful rejection. Another taught me not to trust too soon. And so the lessons go, until I no longer feel "negative charge" with any of them. I exhale with gratitude and relief.

The storm lasts until shortly before sunrise. Even the hairiest experiences I've had in the wilderness were nothing compared to standing up and being pelted with hail, wind, and freezing rain at the top of an exposed ridge for ten hours straight, with soaked clothes and a completely empty stomach. One word encapsulates the physical experience of that night for me: brutal.

In the pre-dawn light, I look around at my circle. My leaf from the Circle of Elders is drenched and tattered, and all four markers of my Medicine Wheel are splattered with mud. My once taut, round rattle is now mushy and mangled into the shape of a warped spoon. I am plastered with red dirt. As I survey the post-storm wreckage, I burst out laughing.

The "grand finale" vision is the sunrise itself. It's spectacular, with fiery purple and orange clouds shaped like airborne swans and eagles. I feel like it symbolizes that I passed the "test" with flying colors.

Before I step out of the circle, I commit my whole being—body, heart, mind, and soul—to my life purpose. I commit with the full awareness that I'll face many, even more difficult storms, now knowing that I have the strength to endure them. I stand undaunted: I'm ready. I'm eager to set off on the path I've chosen, or more accurately, that has chosen me. As the Native Americans saying goes, "The dream dreams you," not the other way around.

It turns out that the point of my Purpose Circle was not to find my life's calling, but to confirm it, claim it, and commit to it.

I pull out my journal from the puddle at the bottom of my backpack, glad that I double-bagged it. Looking out at the clearing clouds as the sun rises higher, I write the last chapter of my book.

Chapter Three
Step Three—Find the Courage to Shine

With your newfound self-love and clarity about how you want to passionately contribute to the world, it's time to make it happen. You are on the last leg of the road to shine: courage and commitment. Many dream big dreams; far fewer make them come true. This part of the journey is the shortest, but it can also be the most challenging.

How do we find the courage to take the leap and

answer the call? For some, it may take a trauma or other major life event, like an accident, losing a job, or getting a divorce. For others, it's a slow simmering of events, feelings, intuitions, and accumulated self-knowledge that motivates them to change their life path to fulfill their purpose.

The nice thing about this stage is that all of your hard work in stages one and two will have paid off, and your life will begin to shift organically. However, fear will never go away. When you take the leap to fulfill your purpose, you will still experience anxiety, ranging from mild discomfort to sheer panic. Nor do the ugly monsters from step one disappear— self-doubt, self-judgment, feeling unlovable, and so on. But once you commit to claiming your life purpose, there's no going back. You can no longer imagine not living your purpose. Anything short of it simply feels wrong. It has become too painful not doing what you're meant to do, where you're meant to do it, with the people you're meant to be with. Thanks to all of your efforts in the previous stages, your courage arises naturally. Your size ten soul finally fits into your size ten—perhaps now even size twelve—dream, and you are walking freely and joyfully upon the earth.

Looking back on my life, I see that we must do the three steps on the road to shine in order, and none of them may be skipped. During childhood, I was clueless about all of the ways that I lacked self-love. So when in college and my twenties, I jumped into steps two and three, courageously living my passions and purpose, it didn't last. I hadn't done the work of stage one, and so I crashed into darkness at age thirty.

I only started down the road to shine when I did the real, in-depth work of step one, uncovering and healing the deep lack of self-love that was holding me back. This vision quest is a culmination of all three steps.

"Thank you, Golden Cliffs. Thank you Death and Rebirth Tree, Circle of Elders, wonderful campsite, and all the spirits of this canyon." I bow in the four directions and gather my soggy, soiled belongings. Elated and full of energy, I practically run back to the base camp.

When I arrive, all the others are already there, breaking their fasts with fresh fruit and oatmeal that Sparrow has waiting for us. Strangely, I don't feel hungry. I sit down, beaming. My group mates look exhausted.

In Native American culture, when a member of the tribe returns from a vision quest, the whole village throws a "welcome home" feast. Afterward, a council of the wisest seniors meets with the quester to help him or her process what happened. Sparrow walks us through how our version of this ritual will work.

"First, you each take turns describing your quests while everyone else listens silently. You can tell your stories however you want: sequentially describing the events of each day, hitting the most meaningful highlights, sharing your experiences as a poem or song . . . whatever you feel moved to do. During this time, there are no questions and no comments; the speaker has the floor. After you all share your stories, it's time to receive feedback from the group. This time, it's the vision quest participant who is silent while the 'elders' each take turns discussing their quests."

After we all share our stories and get comments from the group, Sparrow explains the last stage of our vision quest: "incorporation." Now, we must bring back what we learned on our quests and integrate these lessons into our daily lives. He warns that for some, this will be the most difficult part of the entire vision quest experience.

"A vision quest is done by an individual for the whole community, however large or small you define that group," Sparrow says. "It's not just a soul-searching exercise for your own personal transformation. Whether you physically bring something back or just come home as a better father or sister or role model in the community, you must somehow share what you learned for the betterment of all."

As a last exercise, Sparrow encourages us to write a letter of intent for our "re-entry," including what we hope to accomplish back home and how we will stay centered in our purpose through the trials of daily life. He suggests we call together our Council of Allies, tell them our vision quest stories, and ask them to hold us to the goals we write in our re-entry letter for at least one full year.

Sparrow leaves us with this final bit of advice: "Your goal is to have your daily life circumstances be as close as possible to your life purpose."

⌒

Two days after surviving the hailstorm on the Golden Cliffs, I get up at dawn and look out over Monument Valley. Stumbling out bleary-eyed from the back of my car, I gasp in delight. Below I see a dark, winding road leading up to a brilliant sunrise. The road to shine, indeed.

Now seems like a good time to write my letter of intent. As my vision quest gift to the community, I commit to doing something with my book. I promise myself not to lose heart if a publisher doesn't accept it and to trust that everything will work out the way it's supposed to.

Since I was an "accidental author," I decide to ask my friend Jonathan for advice. His book came out the prior year.

He scoffs, "Laurie, only Moses gets to come down from the mountain and be published." I don't say anything, because I still hope that it's somehow possible.

Over the next few months I do lose heart. The familiar lack of confidence returns: "Who am I to think I can publish a book?"

Then my brother Adam calls me. He mentions that he's going to visit the head of a major publishing company, because she's a fan of his band.

"You know someone from a publishing company?" I ask incredulously. "Would you mind sending her an email, letting her know about my book?"

Within five minutes of receiving my email, Adam copies me on a response from the publisher: "This sounds like a fascinating book. I'm forwarding this email to my top editor in New York."

Minutes later, there's an email to me from the editor, saying she's really interested, asking if I have an agent, and asking me to send her a copy of the book. The whole transaction takes place within the space of ten minutes.

I put my journal face down on my home copier, and make a copy, one slow page at a time. I put the paper copy of my book into a hand-addressed paper envelope and mail it to New York.

Two weeks later, they send me a contract. I am absolutely elated.

I send Jonathan a one-line email: "Call me Moses."

9

Out of the Woods

Climbing the Sand Dune
Stay on Track Even When You Backslide

"Hal is here," my office assistant announces. "He says he has the presentation you're working on together all worked out."

I cringe. Sometimes I dare to push for my own ideas with certain projects but Hal just knocks them down, outlining all of the reasons why they won't work. I don't feel like talking to him right now, but that doesn't matter. It'll be a one-way conversation anyway.

"Tell him I'll meet him in the conference room."

I feel my inner light get a little dimmer.

In the conference room, I find Hal eating his lunch and screaming at someone on the phone.

"Those bastards are so goddamn stupid . . . " he rants, stabbing his fork in the air as his neck veins bulge, his face turning redder and redder. He reminds me of an angry ape I once saw at a zoo. I'm waiting for him to start hurling his feces.

Although he's the one who called me, he looks up at me with an expression of *What the hell do you want?*

When he finally gets off the phone, I say, "Before we start on this presentation, could we look at how we did on the last one? I feel . . ."

"I don't give a damn how you or anyone else *feels*. Got that?"

I had momentarily forgotten whom I was dealing with.

"Um, okay, well, if you have a few minutes, could you review my part of the presentation?"

"I don't have time; I'm really under the gun. Am I the only one here who knows what he's doing?"

"I just thought you'd like to give your input on my slides before I finalize them for tomorrow."

"I said I'm busy."

Just then, a young male intern walks in.

"Ready for that beer? It's barbecue wing night."

Hal grins. "Maybe that hot babe with the big knockers will be working at the bar."

Without another glance in my direction, they give each other a high five and walk out the door.

⌒

Humiliation. Anger. Frustration.

My friends and family keep urging me to quit.

Being in a difficult work situation is similar to being in an abusive relationship. There are so many obvious reasons to leave. With the negativity and disrespect from Hal, I feel beat up. But I care deeply about our company's mission of providing all kids with the chance of a quality education. I keep hoping that somehow things will get better.

I order Chinese take-out for dinner, and my fortune cookie reads, *You have incredible power you are not using.*

⌒

I'm also backsliding in my romantic life. For three years on and off, I've been dating a sweet man named Sean. Sean keeps waffling between pursuing a romance with me and wanting to be "just close friends." In response, I'm neither opening up to him, nor ready to walk away.

"I don't get why you're still with him," says my friend Daisy. "Aren't you tired of his inability to commit?"

"Yeah, but every time I think we're finally done, we get drawn back together. It still feels like we're teaching each other important things about love and relationships."

"Like what?"

I thought about the first time Sean and I had a fight. He said, "Laurie, I know that you're angry with me, and we're going to work this out. But before we do, I want you to know that I love you."

"He's always good about keeping things in perspective. He's also supportive of who I truly am, including my woo woo side."

"That's so important."

"I know, right? But there's just no passion there. And I can't trust him completely. He only keeps his word half the time, and sometimes he waits until I bust him before he tells me the whole truth."

"Sounds like a mixed bag of really right and really wrong."

"Exactly."

"So what are you going to do?"

"I don't know."

My assistant buzzes me again.

"Please tell Hal I'm not here."

"No, he's gone. I'm just checking to see if you registered for the Albuquerque conference."

"I don't want to go. You can give my spot to another staff member."

As soon as I decline, I start getting messages from people across the country, urging me to attend. *What's the big deal with this conference? Why is everyone pushing me to go?*

Then it dawns on me. Albuquerque is a few hours from my vision quest site. This isn't about the conference. I'm being called back to the Chama.

Sparrow had mentioned that some people go back and do a vision quest every year, but it's only been eight months, and I don't know if I want to do a solo quest without the support of a group. But I have learned that when my gut speaks, I should listen.

Once again, I set out for the Canyon of the Strong Women.

⌒

Everything is exactly as I left it. My walking stick is leaning against the barbed wire fence, and my rock cairn is still marking the turn-off to what had been my sleeping spot. It's soothing and strange at the same time, like the "Land that Time Forgot."

When I reach my campsite, I feel the warmth and comfort of coming back to a place where I belong. Moved to tears, I greet the Sentinel Tree and each of the little evergreens surrounding my sleeping spot like they're old friends. I call hello up to the Golden Cliffs and down to the Circle of Elders, which now have leafless, white branches. My dialogue with nature begins again.

"Thanks for letting me come back," I say to the Chama spirits.

Of course. We beckoned you.

"Why?"

You've gotten off track.

They're right. In the months following my vision quest, I'd lost my "life map" somewhere between the front seats of the car.

You're here to get back on the path toward your life purpose and to open your heart to true love.

If this is why I've been summoned, it's a darn good thing I've come.

Beneath the Lightning Tree, my last stone pile is still there, shining white quartz chips in the shape of an "L." I kneel before the tree, eager for its insight.

"Why did I backslide?" I ask. "I was so clear when I left here."

Having a vision of where you need to go isn't enough to get there. After looking out over the forest and seeing the path, you need to do the legwork to get to your destination.

"Okay, I get that, but after taking a few steps in the right direction, why did I turn around and start heading the wrong way, or at least sidestep onto a track that I know won't get me where I want to go?"

Did you pay attention to how you were feeling?

"What do you mean?"

When you do what you're supposed to be doing and make the right choices to stay on your path, you'll feel joy. When you don't, you'll feel pain. When you feel light, hopeful, and expansive, you're making a choice in line with your purpose. If you feel heavy and constricted, the choice is leading you off your true path. You must stay conscious of your feelings as you enter the deep woods.

I had let myself go unconscious. With urgent work tasks piling on my desk, I got sucked into whatever most demanded my attention in any particular moment. But I know that we choose how we spend our time; we choose what our priorities are, like how much time to put into unpleasant work tasks versus things that feel more fulfilling.

"Why didn't I set better boundaries? I know better!"

By habit, people slip back into what's familiar, even when it's harmful to them. It's one of the challenges of being human. Why do you think you let yourself go back to old patterns?

"I think I backslid because making such a big change, even one that's much better for me, feels so scary. In my twenties, I was willing to eat ramen and live on a shoestring. But I don't want to do that anymore. What if I fail at this new path and become poor? From past experience, I know when I take a leap, I always land in a better place, but right now, it feels like if I leave this job and don't succeed at my new path, I'll not only be poor, but I'll also be a big, fat failure. I miss the courage of my youth, to just follow my heart and trust that everything will turn out the way it should. When did I become so fearful?"

Be kind to yourself. Think of it as hiking up a sand dune. You're going to backslide as you step, that's just the nature of it, but you're still heading in the right direction. Give yourself time to get up the hill, and rest when you need to. Notice when you're sliding back, and plant your foot more firmly or in a different place next time.

"How do I know whether I should stay or leave my job?"

Don't get stuck in black-and-white thinking. Remember, there are many shades of gray.

"I don't understand."

But then I get it. I don't have to make a choice between staying in a secure job where I'm unhappy and being penniless while pursuing my path. There's an in-between option. I'll ask my board of directors for a leave of absence, then I can focus more on writing and growing my spiritual coaching practice. I can afford to take an unpaid leave for up to two months. While it's not the radical change I sense I ultimately need to make, it's a start. Baby steps are still forward steps.

⌒

Welcome back, the Circle of Elders greet me

"I'm sorry I strayed from my path," I say, looking at the ground. "I know you had high hopes for me."

Everyone gets off track now and again. What's important is that you find your way back.

"I've come to ask about finding my life partner. Specifically, I'd like to know about Sean."

The real question is "What do you want?" *You must be clear about what you seek in your partner and in a long-term relationship. Once you answer that question, you will know when you've found it.*

"I want someone who adores me. A man who has passion—for himself, for me, and for life. I'm just not sure whether Sean will eventually get there, or whether it's time for us to part."

The trees are silent. A breeze lifts the dried, heart-shaped leaves in the center of the ring and blows them toward my feet.

You must allow Sean to be on his own path, without expectations or timelines. Meanwhile, to have what you desire, you must neither search nor settle.

My gut knows I'm settling.

"I should break up with Sean then?"

Listen more carefully to your intuition. You'll know what to do and when. No need to act immediately or set ultimatums. Just keep following your inner guidance.

"When will I find the person I'm meant to be with? I'm afraid I'll be too old!"

You must be patient. This is an important lesson for you: become attuned to proper pace. Learn when it's appropriate to act quickly and decisively to get things done and when to sit back and let things unfold.

Pardon Me
Learn to Forgive Yourself

Although I've only fasted for three days, and it's not yet nighttime, now feels like the right time to do my Purpose Circle. In the past few days, I've learned many valuable lessons and received clear guidance for getting back on the right path and finding my true love. However, I still don't feel joy. This time, as I "call out for a vision," I'll ask how to rediscover and maintain happiness.

When I reach the saddle by the Golden Cliffs, a powerful gust of wind almost pushes me off the ridge. But I'm not complaining—it's better than hail. I draw and enter my Purpose Circle, unsure of what to do or say. I take a deep breath, then shut my eyes. After a few seconds, I'm flooded with painful memories of all of the ways I've hurt other people and everything I've ever done that I'm ashamed of. Each scene stabs at my heart as I relive every moment in excruciating detail.

After several minutes of this, the shame and pain are too much to bear. I collapse to my knees, heaving with sobs. "Oh my God, I'm sorry! I'm so sorry . . . I'm so sorry . . . "

I don't know where my spirit is or how old I am or even what lifetime I'm in. I'm immersed in the remorse of every horrible thing I've ever done.

Enough, the Golden Cliffs bellow. *Get up!*

Wiping my eyes, I rise to my feet.

Stop punishing yourself and living in penance. You must forgive yourself.

"But how can I forgive myself? I've done so many awful things."

Stop holding yourself to such unrealistic standards. What did you realize on your first vision quest?

"That everyone is doing the best they can with where they are on their paths," I say slowly.

Exactly. Cut yourself some slack. You're way too hard on yourself.

My crying subsides. No wonder I wasn't experiencing joy. How could I, when I'm so busy beating myself up?

All the things you have done, the Cliffs continue, *both good and bad, were lessons. Your spirit chose to spend time in those dark places so you would more deeply appreciate the light. You wanted to experience as much pain as possible so that you would understand others when they experience darkness. In this way, you can more effectively guide them back to happiness. Now that you have learned through struggle, you are ready to grow through joy.*

As these realizations hit home, something inside me releases—a heavy burden I no longer have to bear. But one question remains.

"I sense I'm still holding myself back in some way, and that this is preventing me from experiencing consistent joy. But why, and how?"

You are afraid that if you cut loose and set your soul free, you will do horrible things, and that if you don't repress your pleasure, you'll become a reckless hedon. While you have done things you are not proud of, your spirit has evolved. You have come far enough on your path now that nothing but expansive, good things will occur by fully being yourself.

As these words sink in, I finally forgive myself on the deepest soul level. Looking around at the canyon, the sky, and the trees, I realize that everything and everyone is an integral part of me. I'm working with the Universe, as the Universe is working with me. Although I've experienced this feeling of oneness before, for the first time in my life, I now understand with my whole being that I'm not alone.

Until we forgive ourselves, we can never truly feel happy. We have to show ourselves the same compassion we show to those who hurt us. By forgiving others, we forgive ourselves, and by forgiving ourselves, we lift our bitterness toward others.

It's Okay to Quit; Go Find a Better Fit
Leave What Doesn't Work to Find What Does

Sean doesn't take it well when I tell him we're done. Instead, he begs me for one more chance and suggests that we move in together. Over the next few weeks, I have uncontrollable bouts of anxiety and break out in a rash on my face. My body is screaming, "Wrong way!" It's as if all my cells got together and decided, "She's not listening! Fine, we'll throw it in her face—literally."

A month later, Sean buys me an engagement ring for my fortieth birthday. Then he chickens out. I get off the rollercoaster for good this time. In the "reason, season, or lifetime" categories of relationships, ours was an abundant season, one in which I believe both of us blossomed and grew.

When I get back from my leave of absence, I'm bombarded with emails and messages. Many are pressing things that need to be "done ASAP"; some are from upset employees, and several are from Hal, blaming me for things that happened while I was away. Instantly, my spirit constricts. I no longer belong in this stressful, all-consuming environment. It's like living in a house with cats when you're allergic. You take allergy medicine for a long time and do the best you can to cope, but when you go outside into the fresh air and then return, you realize, "I can't breathe in here."

It's often a tricky balance for me between "being here now" and learning from the present moment, versus knowing when the current situation isn't going to get any better, and it's time to move on. Whether in a relationship, job, or new endeavor, I find it tough sometimes to know how long to stick it out. The good news is that eventually, I always know. Either the whole thing conveniently falls apart, or I become so detached inside, my spirit packs up my bags for me, honks from the curb, and screams, "We're late! Let's go!"

I tender my resignation to Charles and my board, then I call Hal.

"I'm stepping off this project—off all of our projects from now on." Softening my voice, I add, "I really appreciate and admire all your work over the years. I wish you all the best."

"Great, sure . . . whatever," he says abruptly and hangs up.

I'm not angry anymore; I feel matter-of-fact and calm. It's clear that Hal never really wanted to work with an equal partner; he likes to be "the Big Cheese." It must have been just as difficult for him to have to share his power as it was for me to fight for mine.

I even feel grateful to Hal. He taught me some critical life lessons. His constant criticism was a mirror for my own relentless inner critic, reminding me to accept and love all of myself, even the parts I feel ashamed of. He taught me to keep my eyes open for competition and to realize that not everyone sees the world through the collaborative, "win-win" lens I do. Most importantly, by repeatedly knocking me down, he helped me learn to stand up for myself.

Just like that, I walk away from a well-paying job at the height of my career and a boyfriend who cares about me deeply. I'm leaving behind everything in my life as I know it. As scary as that prospect felt before, there's no longer any doubt in my mind that I'm doing the right thing.

⌒

Two days after leaving my job and career, I email my New York editor to let her know that I'm ready to start diving into the book full-time. Within seconds, I receive a bounce-back message saying that she no longer works there. After a few brief conversations with my attorney and the publishing company, it's clear that I'll be leaving the publisher too.

For a few hours, I'm in shock. I just quit my job and am ready to do this writing thing for real, and I no longer have a publisher? Does that mean I'm not supposed to publish this book?

I don't doubt my life purpose, but I need to find a different route to get there. I contact my former editor at her personal email address, and she agrees to work with me on a consulting basis.

Trusting that everything happens for a reason and that the right people and situations will present themselves when it's time, I set off down my new path. My first several steps are clear: Stay off the workaholic hamster wheel and focus on my new goals. Have fun. Relax, rest, and heal.

How's that Working for You?
Release Unhelpful Patterns and Cycles

I sign up for an intensive, week-long residential workshop called the Hoffman Process. The workshop focuses on patterns of thinking and behavior we learned from our parents that keep us from feeling fulfilled in adulthood.

"I thought you were just going to hang out and rest for a while," my brother Adam says. "This workshop sounds pretty intense."

"It is. It's just that I've realized there are some attitudes and behaviors passed down from our family that are keeping me from being able to love and be loved. I think this workshop will help me finally break this cycle."

Prior to the workshop, I filled out an inventory of my most common negative attitudes and behaviors. The survey said that you can tell you're perpetuating a family pattern in one of three ways: 1) You repeat the same behaviors or beliefs; 2) You rebel against them ("I'll never be like my mom or dad"); or 3) You attract people into your life who have them. Sometimes, you do all three. Out of a total of 300 negative patterns, I had 294.

To begin the workshop, the leader asks each of us to go around and say how we're feeling. "Many people stay in their heads so much they don't even know what they're feeling," she says. She passes around a sheet of paper listing several dozen emotions in case we need some help.

"Every day, it's important to check in with your feelings. I like to do it first thing in the morning as I'm waking up, asking myself how I'm feeling right now and about the coming day. In fact, it's important to check in often with all parts of yourself: your emotions, your intellect, your body, and your highest self or spirit. Close your eyes and picture them as different entities standing in front of you. Ask your body what it needs, then your mind, then your emotions, then your spirit. You'd be surprised what important information you find out during this simple exercise. Also, whenever there are conflicts between your mind, body, and heart, ask your spirit to facilitate a dialogue to bring them back into harmony."

"Who's that lady with the multiple personalities? Sybil?" I whisper to the guy next to me. He laughs.

Although I'm making fun, I silently give it a try, asking each part of me what it needs in this moment. My mind is skeptical and thinks maybe I should leave. My body is stiff from sitting so long and wants to get up and move around. My emotional self feels nervous but excited. My highest self wants the other three parts to be patient and let things unfold.

"Okay, now everyone go to the back of the room and get a Wiffle ball bat, gloves, a cushion, some paper, and markers. I'd like you to write down each of your negative patterns from your survey, then bash them with the bat on the pillow one at a time."

"Good Lord, I'm going to be here all night," I mumble.

"Feel free to speak or yell or make any other noises you need. Keep swinging the bat and verbalize, no matter what."

At first, I swing the bat half-heartedly over my head, saying only, "I feel nothing."

I keep repeating, "I feel nothing . . . I feel nothing . . . I feel *nothing* . . . I can't *feel*. Oh my God, I *can't* feel! I *can't feel*!"

Repressing emotions is a pattern I picked up from my father. I write it down on a piece of paper and place it on the cushion.

"I'm not going to anesthetize myself again . . . no more masks . . . no more frozen heart . . . I'm not going backwards, goddammit . . . !" I swing the bat harder and harder.

I pick up another paper with another family pattern I wrote down: "Feeling unseen and unappreciated." This one comes from my mother.

Suddenly, I'm a teenager again, in my family's kitchen. I often stayed up late waiting for my dad, who wouldn't get home from work until after midnight. I didn't want him to have to eat alone, so I would come downstairs to heat up his food in the microwave, set his place at the table, and serve him dinner. While he ate, he didn't talk or even look at me. The most he did was grunt and point to his soda when he wanted me to get up and give him a refill. I figured he must be exhausted after such a long day at work.

One night, my sister came down to get a glass of water. Suddenly, my dad came alive. He laughed and joked with her, then teased her when she walked away without hugging him goodnight.

What am I, chopped liver? I thought in pain. I'd been waiting on him hand and foot for years, and he didn't even acknowledge my presence.

I pick up the bat again and center the cushion.

"I matter! I *matter*!"

Over and over I scream those words as I beat the crap out of the pillow, finally collapsing into such convulsing sobs that I can no longer swing the bat.

With each pattern I smash, I feel like I'm crushing another cinder block in the fortress that has been keeping my passionate spirit locked up inside. As I knock down the "walls," I find myself yelling at the top of my lungs, *"Let me out of here!"*

This verbal therapy stuff is certainly cathartic.

Letting go of patterns seems to be a three-part process. First, you have to name the unhelpful belief or behavior you want to release. Then, you need to identify where in your psyche these dynamics are "hooking in"; e.g., are they caused by a deep-seated fear? An old childhood wound? A "shadow" side trait? Or perhaps a family cycle? Finally, you need to physically let go of the old patterns through both internal and external actions. You don't necessarily need to scream and beat them with a bat; you can also do a visualization exercise, so long as you feel a visceral release.

When I was fifteen, I told my parents I didn't believe they loved me. I had just opened a letter from my mom that she wrote as an assignment from the Peer Leadership Program at my high school, in which all parents were asked to send something to their kids. She ended the letter by saying that she and my father loved me.

I called my parents into my bedroom and held up the letter.

"You only wrote that because you had to," I accused them. "You never say that you love me, and you haven't hugged or kissed me since I was a little girl, unless I initiate it. I feel like you've ignored me my whole life. Why should I believe that you love me now?"

Tears trickled out of my mother's eyes. My father stared down at the floor.

"We're this superficial, emotionless family," I continued. "We don't talk about how we really feel or what really matters. We're not exactly cold, but we're certainly not affectionate or close."

After a long moment of painful silence, my mom spoke.

"You were always the easiest child," she explained. "We'd put you in the crib or in the corner, and you'd happily play by yourself. But your sister and brother always needed attention."

As the oldest child, my sister liked to be in charge. She seemed to commandeer my parents' attention as soon as they entered the room. Meanwhile, my younger brother climbed up anything he could find like a mini-Spiderman. My mother got so worried about him falling and hitting his head that she dressed him in protective headgear. He was quite a sight toddling around in fuzzy footsie pajamas and a three-inch thick hockey helmet.

"So just because I didn't fuss or cry it was all right to ignore me?" I asked. All the years of feeling betrayed and abandoned came to the surface. "Parents are supposed to be there for their kids, to take care of them. But you left me to fend for myself." I was crying now, too.

"I guess your sister has always been your mother's chip off the ol' block, and your brother is mine," my dad said quietly.

"Well, where does that leave me?" I asked.

"You're a happy mixture of both?" he suggested.

But I didn't feel like a happy mixture. My worst fears had been confirmed: I was the unloved, unclaimed child. Neither of my parents wanted me.

Looking back now, I can't imagine the shock and pain my parents must have felt at having their teenage daughter tell them she didn't feel loved. I also feel for all the adolescents today who are experiencing the pain and isolation of life with the depth and poignancy that only teenagers can. I certainly appreciate why the "middle child syndrome" is so heavily addressed in modern psychology.

I don't think my parents meant to ignore the child in the middle; I think things just lose their novelty after the first kid, or else they were burnt out. On the upside, I've learned to be very independent and self-sufficient, having mostly done things for myself. Moreover, having to forge close relationships largely outside of the family, I've become skilled socially, getting along well with all sorts of people.

Seeing my childhood pain through adult eyes, I understand that my parents were doing the best they could, as we all do. Both of them were working very hard—no wonder they couldn't always get to all of us. In their situation, I too might have left the easiest kid for last. I also understand now how I interpreted things through my own lens, at times construing things in a way that corroborated my deepest fear of not being loved.

It wasn't part of their parenting style to be overtly affectionate with their children, but over the years, my mom and dad have grown more open. As an adult child, I share more with them about my life and my real feelings than I have in the past. Each time I do, I'm surprised at how helpful and supportive they can be. Recently, we've spent some wonderful, fun vacations together, and we're closer than we've ever been before.

Some spiritual traditions say that we choose the families we're born into, both to learn and teach important lessons. I'm happy with my choice; I love my family very much. I wouldn't trade my experience growing up with them for the world, even the most painful moments. Pain and struggle lead to growth and understanding, understanding to compassion, compassion to forgiveness. May my family also forgive me.

10

La Bella Italia

With no job or relationship to tie me down, there's only one thing left to do: go to Italy for as long as I can afford to stay. "Why Italy?" my friends and family ask. Because Italy is *fun*, and that's what I need right now. Sumptuous food, inspiring art, sensual men . . . . "What's not to love?" as my Italian friend Silvia says. I put all my bills on auto-pay and buy an open-ended ticket to Venice.

Lighten Up
Just Play!

I wake up to the sound of gondoliers paddling beneath my window. Slipping on a cotton sundress, I go outside and walk through the narrow alleys crowded with tourists. After crossing the Rialto Bridge, I notice a handsome blond man and his father playing with yoyos at a market stand where all of the items have a Pinocchio theme.

"Let me teach you how to 'walk the dog,' old man," teases the son in a thick, Australian accent.

"Teach me, my arse," replies his father. "Step aside, and watch the master."

After a few minutes, I can't help myself. "Can either of you do 'around the world?'" I ask.

"Child's play!" grins the son, introducing himself as Todd from Adelaide.

After several minutes of goading them on and laughing, I say, "Well, it's been nice to meet you. May the best man win!"

I'm fifty yards down the cobblestone street before Todd catches up with me.

"Hey, can I ask you a favor?" he asks, struggling to regain his breath.

"Sure."

"I promised a friend that I would bring back the tackiest souvenir in Venice. I've found a couple of contenders, but I could use your opinion."

"Absolutely." I'm flattered this good-looking Australian with the twinkling green eyes would care what I think.

Todd and I spend the next eighteen hours together, getting lost in the back alleys of Venice, taking silly photos of each other, and hanging out by the empty gondolas docked along the Grand Canal, sharing our dreams and struggles until the first rays of dawn rise over the bell tower in Piazza San Marco. By the time Todd leaves at 5:30 a.m. to catch a flight home, I feel like he's one of my oldest friends.

Clutching my sandals, I tiptoe through the darkened lobby of my bed and breakfast. If my first day in Italy is any indication, this is going to be a helluva trip.

"Anch'io mi chiamo Laura!" ("My name is Laura also!"), I say delightedly to the ninety-year-old woman on the wooden bench. I'm staying in Poppi, a tiny medieval village in eastern Tuscany, studying Italian. After our first meeting, I visit Laura each day after class. She's always sitting on the same bench, overlooking the town square.

Laura is the best person I could have found to practice my Italian. She is so open and forgiving of mistakes and seems genuinely excited to talk to someone new. I'm learning more small talk than I ever thought was possible outside of a singles' cocktail party. *"È bello oggi, no? Pensa che domani pioverà?"* ("It's nice out today, no? Do you think it will rain tomorrow?") *"Ho bevuto un orribile espresso stamattina. Ti piace il caffè espresso?"* ("I drank a horrible espresso this morning. Do you like espresso?") Not once does Laura ask me about the American government and our global activities, which I greatly appreciate.

"What do you mean no one makes homemade pasta in Italy?" I ask my host mother, Marcella, one night before dinner.

Both Marcella and her forty-year-old daughter, Elisabetta, are outstanding cooks, which is unfortunate for my waistline. When the olives come right off the tree and the tomatoes right off the vine, it's impossible to say no. But the pasta thing doesn't make sense to me.

"We just don't have time," Elisabetta explains. "We still make the sauce from scratch, but it takes too long to make the dough, roll it out, and cut up fresh noodles. So everyone just buys dried pasta these days. Even most restaurants don't use fresh pasta, or maybe only in one specialty dish."

I can't believe it. You can find more fresh pasta in northern California than you can in Italy. Sensing my disappointment, Marcella goes outside and shouts orders to her three neighbors who are in their usual spots, hanging out and gossiping through their shuttered windows. Next thing I know, there's a small, aproned group in our kitchen, armed with flour, eggs, and a huge rolling pin. Everyone is chattering and laughing, getting covered in flour. Two little girls join us from down the street, thoroughly enjoying watching the adults make such a mess. Marcella lets me press the dough through the pasta machine while she prepares her favorite "quick sauce." With the special ingredient of these women's loving care, it's hands down the best pasta I've ever had.

Before I left for Italy, a friend had asked me to go to a certain cobbler's shop in Florence to buy her a pair of flats. Handing me a photo of the ones she'd lost, she told me that the owner makes one-of-a-kind shoes, but she hoped I could find something similar. She knew the name of the store, Mondo Albion (The World of Albion), but she didn't remember the address.

I love mini-adventures, so I hunt down the shop and walk inside. The small room is chock full of colorful, crazy shoes of all shapes and sizes—thigh-high purple lace-up boots, glittery, star-shaped pumps, pointy-toed zigzag flats, and fur-trimmed, faux snake sneakers. Brightly speckled pieces of leather dangle over whimsically decorated chairs. A man with a long, white beard emerges from the back, dressed in a patchwork outfit made entirely of paper. I'm not sure whether I've walked into a shoe store or the recruitment office for the Italian National Circus.

This madcap ol' guy certainly doesn't have a problem expressing his inner—or outer—freak. Albion is either brilliantly creative or certifiably crazy . . . maybe both. I spend two hours in his eccentric shop, laughing and taking photos of him and his wacky wares. It turns out he does have some brightly painted flats similar to the ones my friend requested, so I buy a pair for her and another pair for myself.

Albion has stayed in touch with me to this day. He emails me photos of his "live art" shows—the last one featured him parading around in face paint among women wearing nothing but leaves.

It's not in my guidebook, but in Rome the key landmark for me is the gelato store across from the Vatican Museum. Each time I go, I get three flavors, because, hey, life is short. Today, just as I'm leaving the shop, in walks the most stunning, well-styled woman I've ever seen, wearing a slinky red dress and six-inch heels. I take it as a cosmic hint. I may never be able to walk in a pair of stilettos, but it's time for me to start dressing up a bit more. "When in Rome . . ." right?

Lili is my first fashion mentor. "*Molto sexy,*" she smiles, tying a bold scarf around my neck to complement my new leather jacket and high-heeled boots. I missed the direct train from Rome to Assisi, so I'm on a two-hour layover in the sleepy town of Foligno. After grabbing my usual morning pastry and *cioccolota calda* ("hot chocolate"—more like thick brown sludge, the way they make it here), I wandered into Lili's small shop at the edge of town. With so much time to kill, I'm able to try on every piece of merchandise in her store, and Lili seems to enjoy using me as her live dress-up doll.

"Wait, I need to give this back," I say, starting to untie the scarf.

"The scarf is a gift, to remember Lili from Foligno." She smiles and waves goodbye as I walk back to the train station carrying my bulky parcels.

That night at the hotel, I receive another round of fashion advice. Three male clerks cluster around me in the lobby, debating whether my sweater should be tucked in or left out of my jeans.

"*No, no, che brutto!*" ("No, no, that's ugly!") exclaims the receptionist, yanking out my wool top.

"*Ma no, è perfetto!*" ("But no, it's perfect!") counters the concierge.

"*Forse ha bisogno di una cintura?*" ("Maybe it needs a belt?") suggests the bellhop.

They continue fussing over me as seriously as if they were famous designers. Suddenly, fashion feels like *fun.*

I try on another low-cut top in a chic Roman boutique, and end up buying a green, Marilyn Monroe-style shirt and a multicolored necklace with baubles that cascade playfully down the plunging neckline. I pick out a short skirt and cropped, wrap-around sweater to complete the outfit.

If the male response is any indication, my new look is a success.

"Mamma mia, you're beautiful!" "Can I buy you a drink?" "Do you want a ride on my scooter?" "What are you doing tonight?" "How long are you staying?" Men of all ages shower me with compliments everywhere I go. Sometimes I feel flattered by all the attention; other times, it feels like I'm being chased by a bunch of dogs in heat. Regardless, at age forty, I feel sexier than I ever have in my life.

⌒

It seems like everywhere I go in Italy, I run into penises. By that I mean I keep stumbling upon phalluses of all sizes, made of all types of materials. While visiting Pompeii, I learn that Italians venerated the male organ as a symbol of fertility and power. Stone phalluses are carved into the walls on almost every corner of that ancient city. The citizens believed that if they touched one, it would bring them good luck. The women used to rub them, while the men would just tap them. Also in Pompeii, I tour the brothel, one of the ruins' most popular sites. Decorating its stone bedrooms and hallways are paintings of men and women in every position imaginable. I take mental notes—just in case.

A few weeks later, a friend takes me to a penis-themed restaurant. The menu is shaped like a well-endowed phallus; drinks come in tall, plastic glasses with testicle bottoms, and all of the pizzas have names like "Scrotum Pie."

I opt for a salad.

After Pompeii, I decide to head south. I'm particularly drawn to Sicily. I take an overnight ferry from Naples to the Aeolian Islands, then a day ferry to the northern Sicilian coast.

A crewmember allows me to go to the top deck to take a photo, where only the captains' quarters are. As soon as they spot me, Captains Giacomo and Rico offer me a cup of coffee and a seat with them at the helm.

"Oh, Mandy!" we all croon at the top of our lungs, as Rico blasts Barry Manilow from his computer. Next comes the Beatles and other old favorites. As if dancing along, two small dolphins leap in front of the boat. The open sea toward Sicily is as bright blue as the sky above us. Rarely have I felt such pure, uncomplicated happiness.

As I disembark, Giacomo and Rico wave goodbye from the top deck.

"Come back soon!" Giacomo shouts.

"In fact, come back now!" Rico laughs, "I'm just about to put on some Cher!"

The Pleasure's All Mine
Unleash the Passion

I've heard that in warmer climates, the people are warmer. That certainly seems to be the case in Italy. The further south I go, both the temperature and the temperaments get hotter.

I'm walking through an outdoor market in Catania, when a couple running a butcher stand break into an argument. In front of all the customers, the man yells insults at his wife. In turn, she begins chasing him around with a cleaver.

"Lasciami in pace, pazza!" ("Leave me alone, crazy woman!") he screams.

"Dì che ti dispiace!" ("Say you're sorry!") she shrieks back.

Many of the bystanders chime in, defending one side or the other. It's really none of their business, but they all have heated opinions.

I laugh with delight. "Hooray . . . *passion!*"

I reach for my camera and realize I'm out of film. I also have a digital point-and-shoot, but I still prefer my old manual Nikon. I spot a small tourist shop across the street.

"Do you sell Kodak 35 mm here?" I ask the elegant, dark-skinned sales clerk.

"I've been working for ten hours straight with no break; can you believe that?" she says. "Not even five minutes!"

"Wow, is that legal?" I reply.

She leans over the counter, grabs my face, and kisses me on both cheeks.

If someone did that in America, they'd probably get arrested for assault. I just love how expressive people are here.

⌒

I like art well enough, but I'm not one to pontificate for hours about the skillful perspective in a painting or to theorize about the artist's intent. That is, until I see Michelangelo's "Statue of David." For over an hour, I stand captivated by the striking, lifelike sculpture, examining it from every angle. I can't take my eyes off the damn thing. The work of a true master has a mesmerizing energy. I even watch the video analysis next to it from start to finish. Twice.

⌒

I can feel his piercing brown eyes on me as I stand in line to get into the Duomo, a spectacular Gothic cathedral boasting the largest brick dome in the world. He follows me inside.

"*Ti piace il gelato?*" he asks, touching my arm from behind. I startle and almost fall into the red velvet rope protecting the altar.

"*Ti piace il gelato?*" he repeats, smiling as he helps me pick up my dropped camera bag.

It's against my better judgment to walk off with a total stranger, but heck, he's tall, dark, and handsome and looks like one of the Italian models I saw in the airplane magazine. And he found my Achilles' heel: ever since college, I've been a sucker for ice cream.

After our gelato date, Antonio keeps calling, asking when we'll get together again. But as sexy as he is, I have a whole country to see. One-night passion is not what I'm looking for. Unless it feels like it could be love, I'm not stopping.

⌒

My Italian friends Silvia and Claudio should win a prize for being the "ideal couple." They can't take their eyes off each other, and they're so supportive of one another; they even quarrel with affection. On my second night in Florence, they invite me to dinner. Halfway through the meal, Silvia tries to serve Claudio more potatoes.

"*No, no, basta!*" ("No, no, enough!") he protests.

"*Ci sono solo tre pezzi rimanenti*" ("There are only three pieces left)," she insists, standing over him with the dish.

"*Non ne voglio più*" ("I don't want anymore"), he repeats, pushing away her hand.

Sitting back down, she says quietly, "*Ma questi sono le tue preferite*" ("But these are your favorite").

Remembering that his wife cooked for him with love, he softens.

"*Va bene, cara, mettile lì*" ("Okay, sweetie, put them there"), he nods, patting her arm and pointing to an empty spot on his plate.

I avert my eyes as they kiss, looking around their cozy kitchen at the many happy photos of them on the walls.

Theirs is the kind of familiar, comfortable affection that only people who truly understand each other share.

One day, I hope to argue with my true love over a plate of potatoes.

⁀

My Italian friend Guglielmo connected me with his college buddy, Alessandro, who owns a vineyard in western Tuscany. I'm greeted at the train station by a sweet, shy engineer-turned-winemaker. We hop into a dusty truck and disappear into the vines.

I arrive at his vineyard just in time for the harvest. It's a whirlwind of activity. Workers wearing yellow gloves scurry down the rows, and throw handfuls of grapes into plastic buckets; women in rubber boots with their hair tied back pick out stems and push the fruit down metal chutes; purple-black juice flows through huge red hoses into massive silver vats; and an entire warehouse is stacked with empty bottles that are waiting to be filled.

"This one is my favorite," Alessandro says, pouring me a glass of one of his specially blended reds. Under his careful tutelage, I discover my passion for food. He takes me to the finest eateries in the area, and we hobnob with some of Italy's most respected chefs and restaurant owners. Everywhere we go, people shake Alessandro's hand and give us the best seats in the house. He's clearly a resident VIP.

The next day, Alessandro asks if I'd like to take a motorcycle tour around Elba. I've never ridden on one before, but touring a Mediterranean island on the back of a bike sounds very romantic. I hop on his BMW and hold on for dear life as we roar around Napoleon's place of exile. My oversized helmet keeps slipping over my eyes, and even with the heavy jacket he lent me, I'm freezing in the blasting wind.

"Isn't this fun?" Alessandro yells back at me.

"Yeah, it's great!" I say weakly, trying to stop my teeth from chattering.

Guglielmo's wife had a hunch that Alessandro and I would be "kindred spirits," and she was right. He and I talk for hours as he shows me around his favorite sites. He's fascinated by my "photographer's eye" and lets me play with my camera as long as I want in the small villages and countryside around his home. Meanwhile, I love watching him manage all of the activities of the grape crush and hearing about his latest struggles and triumphs in the winemakers' world.

One day at lunch, he tells me that he doesn't usually let people get too close.

"But you surprised me," he says, taking my hand. "You parachuted in over my head without me seeing, then tapped me on the shoulder from behind."

I meet his eyes and smile back.

⌒

"Dammit!" I see my reflection and notice I'm getting the same rash I got just before I finally broke up with Sean. *Where am I going wrong this time?*

Alessandro *is* a lot like Sean in how he interacts with me. One minute, the sparks are flying, the next, he just wants to be friends. Just like with Sean, I'm getting hooked on the erratic affection— like a gambler getting addicted to alternating wins and losses. I'm already daydreaming about spending half the year in Berkeley and the other half living in an Italian villa.

One night, two women show up at his place, dressed to the nines. I try not to smirk as I watch from my upstairs window while one of them struggles to navigate the gravel driveway in her spiky heels. I hear them giggling downstairs as they each vie for his attention.

"Ooh, you're so funny!" the blonde one coos. "This wine is delicious," gushes the brunette. Who can blame them? Alessandro is a handsome, wealthy, single man, a perfect candidate for *The Bachelor*. "Laura, come join us!" Alessandro calls out. Another peal of laughter wafts up the stairwell. Patting concealer on my face, I decide to leave on the next possible train.

⌒

"Have you eaten yet?" asks the nearly toothless old man, approaching me at the fruit stand in San Vito Lo Capo. "Come, come, my wife and I are just starting." He speaks to me in a combination of broken German, Italian, and Sicilian dialect, but somehow, I understand him.

I've just walked off the beach wearing my bikini and sarong. Since the sun has gone under a cloud, it seems like a good time to grab a quick piece of fruit for lunch. Instead, I spend the next three hours with an adorable eighty-something year-old couple, looking at photos of their grandchildren and doing my best to read poems from the heavy, bound book they place on my lap. I'm sure I bumbled the words—the Sicilian language is quite different than traditional Italian, and in its written form, doesn't contain vowels. The old man doesn't seem to mind my faulty pronunciation, though. Clasping his hands together gleefully and flashing his wide, jack-o'-lantern smile, he declares proudly, "I wrote those!"

The two of them are adorable together. They told me they've been together since they were very young kids. He pinches her leg and compliments her beauty, and she listens intently to each word of his poems, although I'm sure she's heard them a hundred times.

⌒

"What is there for dessert?" I ask the waiter at the restaurant in the hotel where I'm staying in San Vito. "Do you have almond cake or gelato?"

Mi dispiace ("I'm sorry"). We have only the fruit bowl left."

"I guess I'll just skip it," I say, disappointed.

A few minutes later, he comes back carrying a large bowl of ice cream. "Compliments of Tony," he nods toward the kitchen. An older man in a chef's hat waves at me.

After emptying the bowl, I lick my finger and write on the bottom, *"Grazie, Tony!"* with a big smiley face.

From that moment on, my friendship with Tony is official. Every evening at the restaurant, he makes me something special. Every night after his shift, we stay up late chatting in the lounge. He tells me all about his childhood and how he met his beloved wife. He gives me sage advice on men and relationships and warns me that I should court for a long time, until I'm sure I've found "the One."

"You sure know a lot about life and love," I say on our last night.

"For Italians, they're the same thing," he grins.

Tony's right. In Italy, the whole country is alive with passion, in their approach to everything: love, food, art, fashion, nature, wine. For them, passion is a vehicle for creativity and joy, paramount to living a full life.

It's interesting that American society applauds passion for work or for a cause, but not passion for pleasure's sake. Pleasure has been given a bad rap as something selfish or "dirty" and is repressed in many places in the world. As a result, many people now use their heads to guide them in their lives, rather than allowing themselves to just *feel*. As kids, we were so open, constantly expressing our every emotion. As adults, many of us have lost the ability to give up control.

I'm not advocating ignoring our rationality and following only our impulses and desires. What I'm learning in Italy, though, is how to regain balance between the emotions and intellect, erring, if anything, on the side of allowing passion to take the lead for a change.

Over the past two months, I've gasped at the beauty of a painting and been moved to tears by the colors of a beautiful sunset. I've had food that made me moan aloud, and I've drunk wine that made my toes curl. Without judgment, fear, or criticism, I'm blissfully vulnerable, letting it all out and taking it all in. I've discovered that the secret to passion is giving ourselves permission to let go.

How to Be Happy Even When Life Is Crappy
Choose Joy

"*Che brutto giorno!*" ("What an ugly day!") exclaims the hotel maid, dragging on her cigarette as she looks out at the pouring rain. Rosario and I disagree. Laughing as we splash through puddles, we jump from doorstep to doorstep, stopping to embrace and kiss under each dry alcove. We arrive at his car, crank up the stereo, and dance and sing while the storm crashes all around us.

An ugly day? Not at all. This is one of the best days I've had in a while.

Ever since we met in Isola Bella, I've been struck by how happy Rosario is. Rowing a boat across the tranquil, turquoise bay, he tells me how much he enjoys his job, appreciates his family, and loves living by the sea. He could view his life differently: "I'm almost thirty and still single, and my job takes me away from my family and friends." Instead, he sighs contently, "*Il mio cuore è veramente pieno di gioia*" ("My heart is truly full of joy").

At first, I think he may just be simple-minded: How can someone be so upbeat all the time? But as I get to know him, I realize his happiness is genuine. He lives fully in each moment, appreciates the small things, and often bursts into spontaneous play.

In one week, I've learned more about true joy from this young Sicilian than I have in my entire life so far. The guy has simply decided his time on this planet is going to be fun. He's not naïve to the struggles around him, nor free from struggle himself. He just chooses to approach life with a positive attitude.

Somehow, we've convinced ourselves that joy is something we have to spend a lifetime working toward. But even by diligently chipping away at our negative habits and thoughts, we might never get a piece of that all-elusive happiness.

What if it's a lot simpler than that? What if it's a lot more fun? What if, like Rosario, we decide that happiness is possible *right now*? Horrible rainstorm or private dance party? My decision.

⌒

On our last night together, I get dressed up in my favorite new outfit from Lili's shop. As I walk down the hotel stairs, Rosario exclaims, "*Mamma mia, sei splendida!*" ("My God, you are splendid!")

If it weren't for the tears in his eyes, I might have laughed. "*Splendida*" seems like such an odd word. Then I realize it comes from *splendere*, to shine. How perfect.

I am indeed shining by the end of my trip. The Isola Bella locals often remark how I'm "glowing."

I came to Italy to find passion and joy. I'm happy to report I found both—not only in that magical place, but more importantly, within myself. I also found peace, which I didn't even know I was looking for.

Epilogue

For all their encouragement about living my purpose, none of the Chama spirits warned me how difficult it can be to follow your dreams. Well, all right, they warned me, but I guess I thought the toughest part would be finding the courage to take the leap. I had no idea that was only the beginning, and that it would take even more guts and grit to see things through.

The transition to my new life was lasting longer than I thought it should. It was taking everything I had to stay positive and hopeful, to be patient and keep the faith when I couldn't see what was coming, to not worry about money, and to find the energy to keep going for as long as it took. *When is my desert vision going to fully manifest? And while I'm asking, where the hell is my Mr. Right?* It made me understand only too well why so many people give up and settle.

But I knew I'd never forgive myself if I quit. I couldn't *not* keep going. I committed to clawing my way out of that pit and to keep taking one step at a time toward my goals.

Today, seven years after sitting in that opening vision quest circle, wondering, *Why am I here?* I'm happy to report that I'm joyfully living my passion and purpose. By staying in trust, I found a wonderful new publisher for my book, began a fulfilling new wellness career, and am finally ready to meet my true love. I realize now that my purpose has been manifesting this whole time.

As I discovered at age sixteen, life is a quest. Harvard, traveling, my education career, the desert fasts . . . all were critical steps bringing me to where I am now. I'm proud of how far I've come— and for someone with a long history of deep lack of self-love to say she's proud of herself, that's a very big deal. I'm proud of *everyone* who's gone through significant pain and come out a better person.

Life is still a big question mark, but instead of it feeling like a scary, dark drive, now I'm loving the open road. I no longer feel the need to see around the next bend to know I'm going the right way. I have a good roadmap—the three steps to shine—and if I ever find myself getting stuck in any of the steps or settling for less, I know how to reset my GPS toward the life I deserve.

So for those of you who haven't yet embarked on your road to shine, or those who've taken the big leap, but whose dreams are yet to come true: *Do it*—then *keep going*.

The world is waiting for your gift.

Notes

[1] John A.T. Robinson, *Honest to God* (Philadelphia: The Westminster Press, 1963), 103.
[2] Mahatma K. Gandhi, *The Collected Works of Mahatma Gandhi—Vol. 91.* Supplementary Volume I (1849–1928). (Publicantion Division, Ministry of Information and Broadcasting, Government of India, 1989), 324.

Bibliography and Suggested Reading

Behrendt, Greg, and Ruotola-Behrendt, Amiira. *It's Called a Breakup Because It's Broken.* New York: Broadway Books, 2005.

Behrendt, Greg, and Tuccillo, Liz. *He's Just Not That Into You.* New York: Simon & Schuster, 2004.

Bethards, Betty. *The Dream Book.* Petaluma, CA: New Century Publishers, 1983.

Cantwell Smith, Wilfred. *Religious Diversity.* New York: Crossroad Publishing, 1982.

Cantwell Smith, Wilfred. *Towards a World Theology.* Philadelphia: The Westminster Press, 1981.

Carter, Christian. *Catch Him and Keep Him.* E-Book, www.catchhimandkeephim.com, 2007.

Casey, Caroline. *Making the Gods Work for You.* Audio CD series. Sounds True, 2009.

Chödrön, Pema. *From Fear to Fearlessness.* Audio CD series. Sounds True, 2003.

Chödrön, Pema. *Getting Unstuck.* Audio CD series. Sounds True, 2005.

Chödrön, Pema. *Good Medicine.* Audio CD series. Sounds True, 2006.

Chödrön, Pema. *No Time to Lose.* Boston: Shambhala Publications, 2005.

Chödrön, Pema. *Start Where You Are.* Boston: Shambhala Publications, 1994.

Clifton, Donald O., and Nelson, Paula. *Soar With Your Strengths.* New York: Dell Publishing, 1992.

Cohen, Alan. *A Deep Breath of Life.* Carlsbad, California: Hay House, 1996.

The Dalai Lama. *For the Benefit of All Beings.* Boston: Shambhala Publications, 1994.

Dyer, Wayne. *The Power of Intention.* Audio CD series. Carlsbad, California: Hay House, 2007.

Eisler, Riane. *The Chalice and the Blade.* New York: HarperCollins, 1987.

Feynman, Richard. *The Character of Physical Law.* Cambridge, MA: The M.I.T. Press, 1986.

Ford, Debbie. *The Best Year of Your Life Kit.* Carlsbad, California: Hay House, Inc., 2005.

Ford, Debbie. *The Dark Side of the Light Chasers.* New York: Riverhead Books, 1998.

Ford, Debbie. *The Right Questions.* New York: HarperCollins Publishers, 2003.

Foster, Steven, and Meredith Little. *The Trail to the Sacred Mountain: A Vision Quest Handbook for Adults.* Big Pine, CA: Lost Borders Press, 1984.

Frankl, Viktor E. *Man's Search for Meaning.* New York: Simon & Schuster, 1984.

Fulghum, Robert. *All I Really Needed to Know I Learned in Kindergarten.* New York: Ivy Books, 1986.

Gandhi, Mahatma K. *All Religions Are True.* Bombay: Bharatiya Vidya Bhavan, 1962.

Gilbert, Elizabeth. *Eat, Pray, Love.* New York: Penguin Books, 2006.

Gilligan, Carol. *In a Different Voice.* Cambridge, MA: Harvard University Press, 1982.

Gray, John. *Men are from Mars, Women are from Venus.* New York: HarperCollins Publishers, 1992.

Harvey, Steve. *Act Like a Lady, Think Like a Man.* New York: HarperCollins Publishers, 2009.

Hay, Louise. *Totality of Possibilities.* Audio CD. Carlsbad, CA: Hay House, 2005.

Hicks, Esther and Jerry. *Ask and it is Given.* Carlsbad, CA: Hay House, 2004.

Hoff, Benjamin. *The Tao of Pooh.* New York: Penguin Books, 1982.

James, William. *The Varieties of Religious Experience.* New York: Longman, Green, and Co., 1902; reprint ed., New York: Penguin Books, 1986.

Kornfield, Jack. *A Path with Heart.* New York: Bantam Books, 1993.

Lamott, Anne. *Traveling Mercies: Some Thoughts on Faith.* New York: Pantheon Books, 1999.

Maitri, Sandra. *The Spiritual Dimension of the Enneagram.* New York: Jeremy P. Tarcher/Putnam, 2000.

Millman, Dan. *The Life You Were Born to Live.* Tiburon, CA: HJ Kramer, 1993.

Millman, Dan. *Way of the Peaceful Warrior.* Tiburon, CA: HJ Kramer, 1984.

Moore, Thomas. *Soul Mates.* New York: Harper Perennial, 1994.

Myss, Caroline. *Sacred Contracts.* Audio CD series. Sounds True, 2001.

Myss, Caroline. *Self-Esteem.* Audio CD series. Sounds True, 2002.

Orloff, Judith. *Positive Energy Practices.* Audio CD series. Sounds True, 2006.

Palmer, Parker. *Let Your Life Speak.* San Francisco: Jossey-Bass, 2000.

Peck, M. Scott. *The Road Less Traveled.* New York: Simon & Schuster, 1978.

Redfield, James. *The Celestine Prophecy.* New York: Warner Books, 1993.

Redfield, James. *The Celestine Vision.* New York: Warner Books, 1997.

Redfield, James. *The Tenth Insight.* New York: Warner Books, 1996.

Reiser, Paul. *Couplehood.* New York: Bantam Books, 1994.

Resnick, Stella. *The Pleasure Zone.* Berkeley, CA: Conari Press, 1997.

Rinehart-Phillips, Vessa. *Opening the Third Eye.* Penryn, CA: Personal Transformation Press, 2005.

Robinson, John A.T. *Honest to God.* Philadelphia: The Westminster Press, 1963.

Ruiz, Don Miguel. *The Four Agreements.* San Rafael, CA: Amber-Allen Publishing, 1997.

Sams, Jamie, and David Carson. *Medicine Cards.* New York: St. Martin's Press, 1988.

Stone, Douglas, Bruce Patton, and Sheila Heen. *Difficult Conversations.* New York: Penguin Books, 1999.

Virtue, Doreen, and Lynette Brown. *Angel Numbers.* Carlsbad, CA: Hay House, 2005.

Walker, Brian Browne. *The I Ching or Book of Changes.* New York: St. Martin's Press, 1992.

Weisskopf, Victor F. *Knowledge and Wonder.* Cambridge, MA: The M.I.T. Press, 1983.

Welwood, John. *Perfect Love, Imperfect Relationships.* Boston: Trumpeter Books, 2006.

Wilde, Stuart. *Silent Power.* Carlsbad, CA: Hay House, 1996.

Williamson, Marianne. *A Return To Love: Reflections on the Principles of A Course in Miracles.* New York: HarperCollins, 1992.

Williamson, Marianne. *A Woman's Worth.* New York: Random House, 1993.